BARBADOS DIARY

MARK BADINSON

Copyright © Mark Badcock 2009

CONTENTS

Introduction 1

Chapter 1   'Oh, We're Going To Barbados' 3

Chapter 2   St Lawrence Gap 15

Chapter 3   Bridgetown 27

Chapter 4   Aloe Vera 33

Chapter 5   A Day At The Zoo 39

Chapter 6   Flight Of The Navigators 51

Chapter 7   Sandrift 57

Chapter 8   Around The Bend 63

Chapter 9   The Flower Forest 69

Chapter 10 The Beach At Holetown 83

Chapter 11 Millions Of Raindrops 93

Chapter 12 The Wildlife Reserve 99

Chapter 13 'We Do Like To Be Beside The Sea' 119

Chapter 14 'Parting Is Such Sweet Sorrow' 131

Chapter 15 Fear Of Not Flying 139

Chapter 16 Return Of The Natives 147

Acknowledgements 155

INTRODUCTION

I guess you could say I was a little bit of an adventurer; I'd travelled abroad a few times on my own, to see what the rest of the world was like. I travelled light and approached everyday with an open mind, no expectations, and enjoyed going on uncomplicated expeditions. The challenge of the unknown and unexpected, that's what I liked in my holidays. It was all about walking or taking public transport from A to B; I'd rather be catching a bus to a place that looked interesting in the visitor's guide, than sunbathing on a beach or by the hotel pool.

In the past I'd done okay on my own. Twelve years ago, as a young single man, I went to Barbados, a popular pocket paradise in the Caribbean. It cost me two hundred pounds--including the ticket--for a week. What could be simpler? Nothing of course (how do you think I was able to do it?). Now, as a married man with two children, I was planning a second visit to Barbados. This time I wouldn't be alone. Joining me were: my two daughters, Michelle (10yrs), Sarah (5yrs), and my sister, Dawn (eleven years younger than me--she's 27). Although there were three other people to think about on this occasion, I didn't expect the holiday to be any different from what I was used to. The first time I was in Barbados I really enjoyed myself; so I'm assuming I will this time--after all, it's easy enough when you're there for the adventure.

Chapter 1

'OH, WE'RE GOING TO BARBADOS'

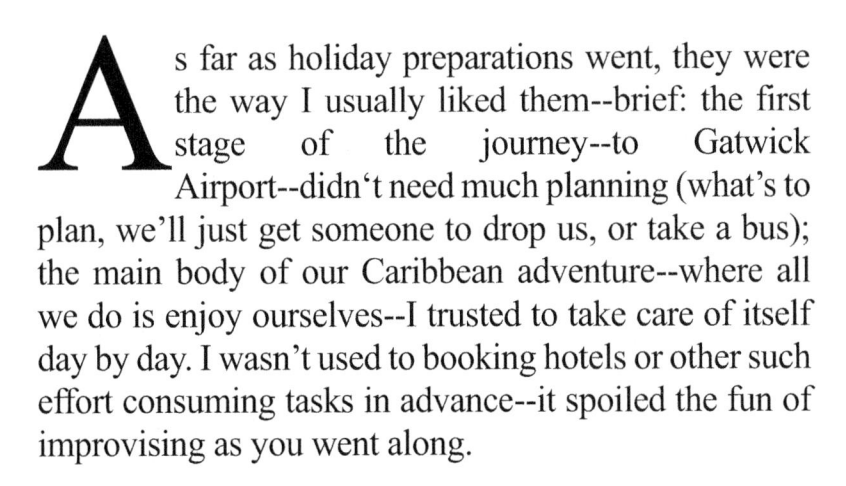

As far as holiday preparations went, they were the way I usually liked them--brief: the first stage of the journey--to Gatwick Airport--didn't need much planning (what's to plan, we'll just get someone to drop us, or take a bus); the main body of our Caribbean adventure--where all we do is enjoy ourselves--I trusted to take care of itself day by day. I wasn't used to booking hotels or other such effort consuming tasks in advance--it spoiled the fun of improvising as you went along.

One fine October morning we began our departure for warmer climes.

The final pre-flight plan simply called for me to drive Michelle, Sarah, and myself, the few miles from our house to Dawn's flat, opposite Hillingdon

Chapter 1: 'Oh, We're going to Barbados'

Hospital. I had arranged to pick Dawn up at 0800hr. From my sister's flat, we'll move swiftly on to brother Ian's palatial residence in toffee nosed upmarket Iver, Bucks; parking the car outside for the duration of our holiday, before my brother (who is five years younger than me) takes us to Gatwick Airport in his sporty little black escort.

Unfortunately my wife Mercy could not come with us because her new job did not allow leave entitlement yet. So on the way to Dawn's flat, I dropped Mercy at the bus stop. We can't all be on holiday at the same time; someone has to go to work. Today, it's Mercy who's working and I'm the one going to Barbados. Such is life. Look, it's just a little island in the Caribbean, no big deal. If it was me not going, I'd accept the situation straight away. But as I am going, I might as well enjoy it; what a great holiday; fantastic Barbados; lots of sun, food, rest and relaxation--better than working. We bid Mercy a fond farewell and promised to send a postcard.

Later, with Dawn aboard and everybody primed and ready to go, I sped past the gothic style Civic Centre building in nearby Uxbridge, in my sort of gold Vauxhall (though it has also been described as silver or even pearly in colour. I always thought it was a shade of brown really...), soon reaching the mini-roundabouts and semi-rural country charm of Iver, where my brother and his family lived.

We waited like coiled springs on the doorstep in the early Sunday morning October light. I tapped gingerly on the bungalow door. Presently, an unkempt, sleepy eyed figure appeared. It was Ian, looking as if--above all else--he wanted to go back to bed. Normally I couldn't blame him, but today was different. Ian had promised us, we were relying on him--and waiting expectantly outside his house for a trouble free start to our holiday.

Luckily, whatever he looked like, Ian was true to his word, and in minutes had positioned himself behind the steering wheel; albeit, half alert with matchsticks holding up his eyelids. I quickly joined the others squeezing into the little escort. The world was our oyster; we were off to a good start and the future looked bright through my rose tinted glasses. The world according to Mark wasn't such a bad place to live (well I didn't think so anyway). My brother's wife, Julie, and little daughter, Lucy, sublimely oblivious to these rude awakenings and surreptitious goings on, were still fast asleep in bed.

To our eternal gratitude and deep appreciation, Ian, despite feeling the effects of an unwanted early morning wake up call, began burning rubber on the road to Gatwick Airport. You should never under estimate the importance and usefulness of your family (I know I don't). I fully intended to be useful myself one day, and it's the thought that counts. We'd only gone around the corner, when our chauffeur decided to stop for petrol. Ian explained it would be at least twenty pounds worth to Gatwick and back. Of course, I was only interested in the journey to the airport. Dawn gave our brother ten pounds (Dawn and I were later to share everything fifty-fifty, but that agreement

Chapter 1: 'Oh, We're going to Barbados'

hadn't been made yet) and after a trouble free ride, with plenty of conversation--some of it from Ian and Dawn--we arrived at Gatwick early. Ian put Bluebird in the short term car park, and the five of us walked over to the departure terminal entrance.

I quickly found BA staff travel, and lingered expectantly a few feet from the desk. Although British Airways employees like myself were able to obtain discounted flights, there was another less shiny side to the coin. The flip side here was, I didn't actually know for sure if we were going on holiday at all yet, as our status was stand by; except for Dawn, who had a firm ticket and could wave goodbye to us now, if she so desired--skipping merrily through passport control and beyond (even sniggering smugly into the bargain if that appealed to her). In our case, being stand by meant that if a lot of people wanted to go to Barbados today, we wouldn't be able to get on the plane.

Ian and Dawn supped in obvious satisfaction on thin weeds rolled up in white paper and lit at one end--an abhorrent habit. Meanwhile I waited with bated breath. So bated was it--a fox and two badgers were sniffing around me and tugging at my trouser leg. The last time I saw a badger was also in front of a staff travel desk (wild eyed beggars unashamedly badgering the travel desk royalty for a glimmer of hope, the tiniest sliver of possibility so they could leave off applying the Grecian two thousand for at least a few brief moments). These were worrying times, the minutes seemed like hours--they probably were. The furrows in my forehead grew more pronounced by the second. Suddenly, calm and tranquility descended, all concerns vanished into thin air; gradually, my mind relaxed like David Carradine's mentor in the Kung-Fu series, when he says "ah, grasshopper" as I became only the second of the stand by staff to be called forward. I was using my free flight, and fortunately it had priority status above the normal 'don't ring me, I'll ring you', park bench and old newspapers ticket.

Bubbling over with joy, trying to contain my happiness, I took one look at the anguished (the kindest word I can think of...) faces, staring feverishly at the counter. In red rimmed eyes, tears welled up, finger nails dug into suitcase handles; while in the background, an entire orchestra of violins played slowly and sarcastically (and hurtfully) 'Leaving On A Jet Plane'. These people make me sick! They should be strong, accept the situation. There are worse things in life than turning up to go on holiday and finding out at the last minute--you can't go. Look at me, I accepted my situation straight away.

Those still waiting, watching forlornly with puppy dog begging eyes, and constantly whimpering voices pleading for a chance to go on holiday, stood strangely, their faces taking on a lunatic expression as lopsided smiles spread across their light green faces. How sad for such unfortunates, who continued to stand by and hope their luck came in. Giving not a second thought to these people, I went over excitedly to tell Ian and Dawn we were on.

Dawn, myself, and the children, said goodbye

Chapter 1: 'Oh, We're going to Barbados'

to Ian, before walking through passport control. Dawn pointed out our seats were all in non-smoking, and henceforth her life would be hell on the flight. She told me frantically, that there were smoke alarms in the toilet, and you couldn't get up and have a smoke standing. Dawn would get no pity from me on this issue. Maybe the cabin crew could supply a bit of leather she could bite into.

As we approached the duty-free shops, I began to walk a little faster--for it wasn't long now to departure. Dawn said she needed to buy some cigarettes--would I wait for her? The seconds ticked by, and I began to get impatient, walking further away towards the tunnel that led to our boarding gate, now and again looking back to see if Dawn was coming. Finally, she caught us up and we went quickly along the tunnel.

At the boarding gate, everybody was going on to the plane. Dawn, myself, and the children were checked through by, what at first appeared to be a sympathetic woman, who commented that it was a pity we were all split up on the aircraft. I had walked on a few yards, when her voice called out--unnecessarily--after me: "anyway, you're lucky to get on..."

She might as well have said: "hey everybody, they didn't pay much for their tickets--they're only stand by staff!"

Stepping onto the plane, I pointed out to the middle-aged looking stewardess (I'm sure she wouldn't mind me saying that) our party were split up;

and my youngest daughter, being only five, would not feel very happy sitting on her own (unlike my oldest daughter). The stewardess (middle-aged one) said she would pass a message to the cabin staff working in our section of the aircraft.

Once in the seat, I decided to keep Sarah on my lap. The stewardess gave me a child safety belt to attach to my own seat belt--although she did think Sarah was a little big. It was unusual for anyone to call Sarah big. After a couple of hours, this arrangement began to get uncomfortable. As dinner time approached, experience told me the situation would become decidedly more difficult. So far, Sarah had been very well behaved. There was only another six hours to go. Dawn indicated to me--from her seat to the right, about five rows in front--Michelle was happy (I suppose this was achieved by smiling and pointing, I don't quite remember). Michelle was in a window seat to the right of Dawn and about two rows behind. At least we were all in the same section--though I wouldn't have minded being in first class. A stewardess eventually came over to me, and said that a middle-aged couple sitting in the middle row (one of who was actually sitting next to Sarah's empty allocated seat), had offered to split themselves up, so that Sarah and I could have two seats together. The lady took my seat, and we all settled down ready for our first meal.

Although the couple were staff also, it was still kind of them to help us out. This exchange of seats was only supposed to last for the duration of the meal, but the couple thoughtfully let us stay there for the whole flight. I did quite well, as Sarah didn't eat much of her food and it gave me the opportunity to have two of everything; but the chocolate mousse with chocolate sauce twice, may have been a step too far.

The worst thing about flying, I find--besides being there--is turbulence. If some should happen along and you're like me, possessing a seemingly easily sickened physique, then prepare yourself for a roller-coaster ride on the big dipper. My memories of turbulence sickness are most unpleasant; especially when I remember that while you suffer in heroic silence as much as possible, no-one can do anything to help you. The cabin crew offer only peeled back lips and an occasional panoramic view of their white, tombstone sized teeth with a touch of false sympathy thrown in. You, dear friend, paid £700 to be strapped into a small seat for eight hours--with no avenue of escape. There is some consolation for me in not having to pay £700, but when I'm suffering like that, whether I paid for it or got it free doesn't make any noticeable difference. Fortunately, the flight out contained only a few short instances of this unwelcome pain in the airs, and my vomit threshold remained untested.

Sarah, eating so many peanuts I said she would look like a Barbadian peanut (this was before I knew the indigenous people of the island were in-fact properly referred to as Bajans), behaved herself very well considering it was an eight hour flight. There were activity packs provided for children, which helped Sarah pass the time. My youngest daughter's only real misdemeanor was knocking over a full glass of orange juice. Some of the orange went over me, but most of it went into the lap and down the shirt and one trouser leg of our kind friend, who had changed seats earlier. I wonder what he thought of us now (so this is how they pay me back). Although reacting like a herky jerky rag doll initially, he didn't seem to mind too much before leaping up quickly and hurrying off to the toilet. Now I had to order another orange juice.

Michelle was happy enough sitting on her own. Every now and then she came over to see us. Dawn though, had one or two problems. It was common knowledge she must have a seat in the smoking section to survive, but as British Airways (called something quite different by Dawn now, I should imagine) had not given her one, she suffered some discomfort during the flight. It appeared at first Dawn would be able to change seats with someone in 'smoking' at the back of the plane. But her watermelon sized smile turned into a scowl of derision, when for some unknown reason, this more suitable arrangement was cold-heartedly cancelled.

Eventually, fate extended a comforting hand to our unhappy mortal by providing her a place of temporary refuge from the clean air that must have been threatening to infiltrate every part of her lungs. As we dipped slightly to avoid air currents, at the rear of the aircraft--near the toilets--a huddled figure could be seen drawing breath on a short, white, rolled up piece of paper dimly glowing from the opposite end.

Chapter 1: 'Oh, We're going to Barbados'

For Dawn, life had begun to look sweet once more. Occasionally, the odd wet shoe would brush against her, as another satisfied customer made an awkward exit from the shoe cupboard size toilet cubicle. No doubt somewhere far below us (assuming we were not over the sea, how would I know, sitting in the middle rows?) in some city street, a down and out was scouring the alleyways and dustbins for a morsel of food--or better still, an unfinished cigarette butt. Dawn was not alone.

For hours, Sarah had been asking me if we were in Barbados yet. Well, now I could answer yes--as in a few minutes we would be. My first impression, looking towards the window as our wheels touched down, was that it reminded me so much of the Philippines, with its sparse green landscape, blue skies and unsophisticated buildings.

In a short while, our passports had been processed. Standing bleary eyed in the baggage reclaim area, Dawn and I stared at the conveyor belt--expecting as did everyone else, that the first bags to appear would be ours. Michelle thought she saw them, but of course they were not there yet. When at last, our baggage did arrive; I took the two heavy pieces and led the way past a bank, through customs and out into the daylight world. Unfortunately, there wasn't another bank outside the terminal as I expected (maybe I thought they had built the airport to suit me), so I had to ask the security guard on the door if we could go back in. The guard said 'yes' (they were so happy we'd decided not to stay), and we dragged our luggage past customs, over to a little window tucked away in the corner. The bank's exchange rate was about three Bajan dollars to the pound. Next door to the bank was a tourist information center, with a vast array of pamphlets displayed outside. After studying one of these listing hotels, apartments, and guest houses, Dawn and I selected an abode that met our requirements. The woman behind the desk phoned through and booked the accommodation in advance for us. By the time this business had been concluded, everyone else had vacated the building; it was a veritable ghost town, with me--after that flight--looking like a long time resident.

Outside--for the second time--in the now fading daylight, I employed a mini-cab driver, and we were soon on our way to an apartment in St Lawrence Gap, on the south coast of Barbados, not far from the airport. St Lawrence was located in the main tourist area, with a concentration of accommodations, shops, restaurants, and night clubs. During our drive out, Michelle and I both felt as if we were in good old Philippines--so similar was the climate and our surroundings. Yet in reality, there was about half a world separating the Caribbean from the Far East. After twenty minutes, the cab pulled quietly into St Lawrence. The driver stopped under a sign boasting the words 'Four Aces'.

Chapter 2

ST LAWRENCE GAP

I removed all our luggage from the boot, then, with a sigh of resignation, paid the driver what he mistakenly thought he was worth. We were standing between two wooden apartments; one a bungalow, the other two stories high. In the gathering darkness there didn't appear to be a reception area. The taxi driver pointed further down, where, at the end of the bungalow, there was a little wooden fence joining on to another apartment. Now the driver had his money he didn't want to waste any more time--and disappeared like a thief in the night. Dawn, myself, Michelle and Sarah walked up to a small gate in the low fence. Dawn leaned over, calling out "hello" to whoever might be inside. After a few seconds, a stout old lady appeared in the doorway of the second apartment and asked us to come in.

Chapter 2: St Lawrence Gap

Her home was a modest arrangement of furniture, with family photographs and postcards from abroad pinned on the wall. The old woman told us that so many people who had stayed at her apartments kept in contact and came back every year. I suppose that was meant to be a recommendation, but I'm not so easily fooled (though still easily). Dawn and I were given the keys to the apartment, the first one at the other end of the little fence, opposite the old lady's place. We liked it straight away. There were two bedrooms, each with a bathroom and shower. There was also a nice little lounge adjoining a long narrow kitchen. The kitchen had table and chairs, cooker, fridge freezer, saucepans, plates, cups, glasses, a kettle--in fact, all the necessary cooking utensils for Dawn to do the cooking.

Dawn and I went back to the old lady, satisfied that we would stay at least a day or two. It was then we began to discover what a devious mind she had. At first, the old woman required only two days rent in advance; but when Dawn mentioned we probably wouldn't stay long, she changed her mind and asked for three. Next up came an attempt to have us believe she wasn't sure what the exchange rate was. What? Dawn and I had just come off the last banana boat, so were not exactly familiar with Bajan economics--but we still had a good idea of the exchange rate. In the old lady's case, I do feel that working in the tourist trade and having probably been a resident since the first half of the nineteenth century, she hardly had a ten gallon hat excuse for not knowing exactly what the exchange rate was.

The old fraudster kept asking Dawn how to spell our name, as if she wanted to give us the impression of not being all there and we should feel sorry for her. Now this may well be true--there might be a few sandwiches missing from the picnic--but her mental dexterity didn't seem to be lacking when it came to trying to have us over. And anyway, we were far more likely to feel sorry for ourselves. This vampire bat of an old woman owned the magicians inner circle catalogue of tricks and a well-rehearsed repertoire for extracting as much note or coin possible from unsuspecting guests.

There was a TV in the apartment that apparently belonged to the old lady's daughter, who had forgotten to take it out. If we wanted to use it, there would be an additional cost of six or seven dollars a night. Eight out of ten for that effort. In one room a notice informed cliental they would be charged extra if the air-conditioning was used over ten hours a day, but the old woman told me the limit was eight. Only six out of ten for this--being more obvious. Our reasonably priced accommodation could soon rise drastically to become unreasonable. I gave the old bat a hundred Bajan dollars, which left one hundred and eighty to pay the next day (after we had visited the bank). Dawn and I agreed at this point to split all our expenses fifty-fifty.

The old woman was as tough as two first world war army boots--between her and Robert 'your pension is safe with me' Maxwell, I don't know who I'd trust less. Her 'Wiley Coyote' ways would put a fifty-two card pack of hyenas to shame. I should think that the only person capable of getting out of paying her extra was Houdini (and he wasn't due a holiday in Barbados this year I heard). The world is made up of many kinds of people and old poltergeist features is one of those kinds that make it difficult for the rest of us. Fortunately, I had a secret weapon--Dawn was on my side. Dawn possessed a sort of sixth sense which told her when something wasn't right. I didn't seem to have it myself. Maybe it's because Dawn wasn't stupid.

Dawn and I were both tired from our flight, wanting only to relax now we had somewhere to stay. Firstly though, the small matter of supplies--as we didn't have any. The old lady told me a general store a few yards down the road would be open until 19:00hrs. It was now 19:05hrs, but we went there anyway and the sign outside said 'closing time 22:00hrs'. Maybe the old woman was a few sandwiches short after all, but the impression still remained that under the rhinoceros skin, she was as hard as a suitcase full of six inch nails. I bought a few bottles of seven-up, wholemeal bread rolls, margarine, biscuits, two cans of baked beans, and a small carton of fruit punch for Sarah (very nice). Dawn bought her goods, and then we went back to the apartment.

I switched the TV on once out of curiosity, but finding only one channel with a half decent picture and programme that wasn't even remotely interesting, I quickly turned it off. This brief flickering image would be the first and last TV blip to invade our holiday adventure. There was plenty to talk about, especially the plans for tomorrow. Dawn was feeling a bit rough, but didn't let it get her down too much. Michelle needed a swimming costume, so I said it would be best to go to Bridgetown (the capital) tomorrow and buy one, while having a look round. When the conversation came to an end, it was time to catch up on our beauty sleep (particularly me of course, as I needed it the most).

Gradually, we all sloped off to bed, slept for a few hours, all woke up and then went back to sleep again. I had air-conditioning in mine and Sarah's room, but switched it off about 03:00hrs, thinking not to go over the eight or ten hours. Dawn and Michelle had a big ceiling fan in their room (there was also one in the lounge). I opened all the shutters on the windows, making it pleasantly cool as a slight breeze passed through the room from one window to the other. Luckily, we had wire mesh on each window to keep mosquitoes and similar undesirables out.

The next morning I awoke at 06:30hr and got up soon after. Sounds of early morning Barbados drifted through the open shutters. Outside, Bajans were greeting each other in the street with a constant question and answer of:

"Alright?"

"Alright".

Breakfast for me consisted of a tin of baked beans with some wholemeal rolls and margarine. In a while, Dawn was up too and tucking into a bowl of cornflakes. Sarah wanted cornflakes also; Michelle had toast. Dawn boiled the kettle, and then made us a cup of tea, old chap.

This morning, our first move must be to visit the bank and thereafter pay the old lady--as agreed. I suppose if she had her way, there wouldn't be any funds left over for the rest of the day's activities. When breakfast was finished, Dawn and I picked up our travellers cheques and passports, then, snapping shut the big padlock on the front door, we stepped out into the Barbados sunshine.

It felt so hot; I was glad I had put some of Dawn's sun block cream on my nose. The bank was in a very convenient position--only a few yards away on the opposite side of the road. Inside, we were welcomed by state of the art air-conditioning, which is the case with every bank I've visited in a hot country (at least somebody lives in the lap of luxury).

Before leaving this cool little building, I discovered that if we followed the road further up, past Dover beach, it would eventually take us to the main road--leading to Bridgetown. Here you could catch two types of public transport buses and the smaller mini-buses that went directly to Bridgetown's main bus terminals. I planned to use the buses because they were much cheaper than the taxis, hovering like vultures near our apartment. These birds of prey wanted to rob me of B18 for the trip to Bridgetown, which is approximately £6 (divide by three for sterling), and buses are a standard B1.50 per passenger--so it would be only £2 for the four of us. I would save £4 on one journey, though we'd have to walk a mile first to reach the bus stop (carrying suitcases if we were moving residence). My problem with the money is that I keep thinking I'm dealing with Filipino currency; Bajan currency has twice the value of the peso.

Outside the bank, we decide to take a little walk past the taxis. The drivers beckon us over. They say in false astonishment:

"You can't walk to Bridgetown, are you going on the bus?" Then:

"You can't take those kids on a bus"

I'm sure they have our best interests at heart, but certainly for the time being, I had to decline their gracious offers of transportation with a smile. Thieving vultures.

On the way back to the apartment, Dawn and I are roped in by a young girl calling from the other side of the street. She told us we could enjoy a free ride to a new beach resort being built nearby. There would be a guided tour around the resort, lasting maybe an hour and a half. They'd also give me a free bottle of rum and t-shirt (is that all?). The girl then explained she was going to get paid if we went and it would help her through college. I didn't think she was doing this for nothing. I said we'd be back in about five minutes. It sounded like a good idea and we could go on to Bridgetown after (why, this was a great idea,

Chapter 2: St Lawrence Gap

everything for free, nothing to pay, something for nothing--everyone's dream come true. All we had to do was give up a little of our time).

Two minutes later, Dawn pointed out to me that this girl was probably selling timeshare--they would be expecting something from us in return. My heart sank, jaw sagged, shoulders slumped at the realization free gifts exist only in the minds of children at Christmas. Maybe I still believed in Santa Claus. Dawn didn't want to have anything to do with them. Feeling slightly deflated, I knew Dawn was right. I'd promised to go back in five minutes, which now left me naively thinking I would be letting the girl down. The trouble is, I don't easily see through people; unlike Dawn, who, with seemingly x-ray vision, can find some degree of transparency in anyone. Maybe it's just that she isn't stupid.

A few moments later at the apartment, Dawn says no, she definitely didn't want to go on this timeshare visit. If the girl was still there, just tell her we don't want to go. Dawn went around the back to pay the old swizzer. When she returned, I suggested it would be nice to have a quick look at the beach before our trip to Bridgetown. I told Michelle and Sarah they could go swimming later, if there was time. After locking up once again, we walked along a muddy and debris littered path that opened out onto the beach.

Everything looked okay to Dawn and I--it was sand, it was water. The children were just pleased they had seen the sea. The best was yet to come, for if Michelle and Sarah were lucky, they might get the chance later to go in the water before it got dark. But for now, it was time to head for the main road, from where we could catch a bus to Bridgetown.

Dawn and I tried to creep past the timeshare girl by keeping on the opposite side of the road. This didn't work of course, as she had obviously been watching like a hawk for our return. When the girl made a move to ensnare us once more in her spider web of dialogue, Dawn told her curtly we didn't want to go now. I was behind Dawn all the way here because I thought she would handle the situation better than me. I wasn't scared or anything, but Dawn just had the edge in getting rid of people using a no-nonsense abrupt manner. I usually ended up chatting away with blinkers on, where Dawn would have pointed in one direction, told those concerned where to go and blown smoke after them, narrowing her eyes as she watched the failure slink off without a word of argument.

The timeshare girl simply said: "Okay" and walked away.

Bajan people don't appear to ever get mad if they can't have you over; it's accepted good naturedly. Making little comments to each other is the only usual reaction. I wouldn't be surprised if the girl had already gained some success with these smooth approaches. At the end of the day, her boyfriend probably turned up in his Mercedes to carry them off to their expensive apartment by the beach, somewhere in the upmarket area of St. James.

Chapter 2: St Lawrence Gap

Not having a Mercedes, Dawn, myself, and the children had no choice but to walk to the bus stop; unless Dawn and I were prepared to line the pockets of one of the thoughtful, selfless taxi drivers who now tried to entice us. But they failed again, murmuring little comments as we continued our stroll; in time passing clubs, restaurants, shops and a very nice Dover beach. Finally, I caught sight of the main road. In a matter of minutes, a mini-bus pulled up and we climbed aboard.

Slow, bass heavy reggae music, pulsated through the interior of the bus (and our bodies) as we sped along the road. The passengers are packed in tightly, and it's not a particularly comfortable ride, but for B1.50 a head, they have to make their money (while I save mine).

The route to Bridgetown is about three to four miles, taking us alongside the coastline, through a built up tourist area similar to that encountered on our walk to the main road. When we went past a Kentucky Fried Chicken take-away at a place called Rockley, I said to Dawn, Michelle and Sarah, the Kentucky was opposite a boarding house I stayed at twelve years ago, when visiting Barbados on my own. The old wooden guest house had gone now, replaced by a Texaco garage (I bet the guest house owner--another old lady, aren't they all--made a tidy sum selling up). The Kentucky Fried Chicken would probably be there forever.

Funny, but being tall I couldn't see out of the window properly; it was as if the top half of the picture was missing. Though, even with this disadvantage, the colourful and vibrant images of a passing Barbados I did have sight of, held some fascination for me. Most of the buildings along this coastal route were made of wood. Flashes of green palms and other plants sprang up between. Every so often, the deep blue of the far reaching sea appeared in my frame of view, painting a more complete picture of what the island is all about. At this moment I felt happy to be here. Shortly, our mini-bus arrived in Bridgetown, stopping in a car park sized area, which was half full of queues of other mini-buses waiting for passengers. Further up I could see another parking area, which contained only small yellow buses with blue lines through the middle. I lifted Sarah out and waited for an enthusiastic Michelle and mega cool Dawn (resplendent in shades) to join me.

Chapter 3

BRIDGETOWN

Leading our band of intrepid adventurers (I had longer legs), I headed towards a pathway that cut across a piece of grassland to reach the main road leading into Bridgetown on the other side. The four of us walked up and over a little set of stone steps about halfway down the path. It would have been easier going around them, but I didn't notice at the time and the others just followed me. I turned right at the end of the path, though Dawn said it must be the other way. I was pretty sure, but decided we'd settle the issue by asking some people coming towards us. Not surprisingly to me, I was right, and marched triumphantly, like Napoleon (before he met his Waterloo), into the center of Bridgetown.

Dawn had bought herself a smart and functional

Chapter 3: Bridgetown

hat earlier, to keep the sun from her delicate complexion. I kept trying to borrow it now, as the sun beat down in an unforgiving manner on my own delicate complexion. Dawn's ability to recognize the capital of Barbados when it stared her in the face may have been slightly suspect, but her power to see through people was thankfully unsurpassed (the famous psychiatrist Freud and fictional detective Sherlock Holmes possibly coming a distant second and third). Dawn also had a mean choice in hats. By comparison I lagged woefully behind in these respects; after all, I didn't even have a hat. I could carry heavy suitcases. Maybe Dawn isn't much cleverer than me; it could be she just has more common sense. At least I knew which way I was going.

Barbados itself spans only twenty miles by fourteen wide; correspondingly, Bridgetown is very small as far as capitals go. Since I had been here twelve years ago, there seemed to be a lot more office block and store development. But the little harbour in the center of town, with the bridge on one side--just ahead of us--were as I remembered them. Before the bridge, on our right, was a large bus terminal, where you have to pay at a counter for your ticket (this was not the case for other transport services). Inside I could see two Pepsi machines with a selection of cold drinks. I never saw cold drink dispensers anywhere else in Barbados.

Passing the terminal and crossing over the bridge, we entered the island's main shopping area. I ducked in and out of every dinky little clothes shop along the way, vainly hoping to come across a costume for Michelle. All we could find though, in that line, were racks and racks of men's swimming shorts, interspersed with a few women's swimwear items. Not our lucky day was my elementary deduction.

In the middle of this muddle of a search, Dawn was not feeling too well. She had a headache with a bit of congestion to go with it. We bravely soldiered on. In one shop, I found a t-shirt I liked for B9.95, which was very good value for Barbados. They had the same shirt in teddy bear size to fit Sarah. When she saw it, Sarah wanted one like her Daddy. Michelle was interested in the big baggy trousers, but the shops only had them in men's sizes; at a market place we passed through, she bought two bandanas.

A sense of disappointment began to creep up on me, as the quest to provide Michelle with a swimming costume looked an increasingly more difficult proposition than finding the Holy Grail. But just as others weaker than our iron willed selves would be about to give up, Lady Luck lent a hand. It was the stubby, sun kissed finger of a friendly Bajan native that pointed the way. This local help was very much appreciated, as apparently the place we were advised to try, 'Cave Shepherd', would have what Michelle needed.

Cave Shepherd was only a few minutes away. The best comparison is walking around Southall (a small London town, known as 'little India') and then going into Harrods. Dawn and Michelle quickly went over to the swimming costume section, where there was a large selection. Michelle eventually settled for a strikingly designed suit, that carried a weighty price tag; but it was the one she wanted and Dawn didn't mind paying, she said it was a birthday present from her.

Nearby, there were some quality looking t-shirts, enlivened with pictures of sharks, swordfish, barracudas, turtles, whales--half the ocean population it would seem--all in glorious living colour. None of porpoises though, which Michelle likes, so I bought her a shirt depicting killer whales. Dawn bought three postcards to send home (at least it saved me the trouble). Michelle chose a poignant card showing a very sad little figure with a tear in its eye, saying how much they're missing some one. Who was that for I wonder--what did it all mean?

At the pay counter, the boy with aspirations of being prime minister of Barbados one day, charged me too much on my Barclaycard for the t-shirt. When I shrewdly pointed this out to him, he admitted making a mistake (of course he wouldn't say it was intentional and designed to supplement his income), then began to print out a deduction of that amount to cancel out his error. This genie of the cash register either needed intensive retraining or investigations made into his usage of the equipment, as amazingly, the supposed correction turned out to be incorrect also! Another cancellation was made before 'Fingers Maloney' (the new kid in the cabinet) managed to produce the simple receipt he should have presented to me in the first place.

While this epic of incompetence was unfolding, Dawn stood pale faced beside me, saying she could be sick at any minute. Moving fast, I grabbed a plastic bag from the counter and gave it to her. Dawn asked what it was for--I said for being sick in. Not a nice subject to bring up, but fortunately, at the moment--though wavering and looking a pale imitation of her normally slightly less pale and animated self-Dawn held control over the little nagging voice urging her to act instinctively. If she did lose control, I wouldn't really mind--particularly if it was within my power to direct the unsightly flow over the cashier. We'd be paying him back for some of the inconvenience and it would teach him to keep Dawn waiting when she wasn't feeling well. I came out of Cave Shepherd with about six receipts for one item.

Following this endurance, Dawn needed to sit down for a while and the children were getting thirsty, so we went back to a place we'd been to earlier and liked. Michelle took Sarah upstairs to the toilet. Dawn, sitting as if she'd been ten years in Siberian salt mines on a Spartan diet, looked even more increasingly unwell this sunny afternoon. Hunched forward slightly, Dawn told me in a thin voice--without an enthusiastic bone in her body--she didn't know if she could make it back yet. Dawn peered indifferently from under heavy eyelids and emergency ward ten white face. Luckily for me, we didn't share this fifty-fifty--I felt great!

After doing some shopping in a supermarket,

Chapter 3: Bridgetown

we started walking to the mini-bus park. On the way, one of them stopped alongside us. Although he wanted to rob me of B12 for a ride to St. Lawrence, which is twice the normal cost, Dawn, being desperate to get home as soon as possible, said she'd pay for it. That concluded any dissent on my part (this splitting everything fifty-fifty was going well).

The driver went almost to the Four Aces, thereby saving us a long walk from the main road. Just as well, Dawn wasn't really up to it. Also, the night was closing in and the thought of having to leave Dawn by the roadside if she slowed us down too much, was a constant worry on my mind. Who knows what dangers were lurking in the dark. That's why we had to get back to the apartment quickly--in case anything happened to me.

Chapter

4

ALOE VERA

Soon after returning to the apartment, as it was still a little light, I took the children down to the beach. They had been asking on and off to go swimming, so were really looking forward to actually putting foot to water. Dawn wanted to stay in the room for a while, but said she would join us later when she felt a bit better.

We walked through the muddy, debris littered alleyway, not knowing (this being one of life's little jokes, as if I didn't get enough) that on the other side of the apartment, across the way from us, about thirty yards distant, was a clean, tidy pathway to the beach. A few days later, I discovered it, but to what useful purpose, as at that time our determined group was departing the hospitality of 'The Old Vampire's

Chapter 4: Aloe Vera

Retreat', struggling along the road, suitcases in hand. It didn't matter really because this was the only time we would visit that beach while staying at The Four Aces.

Michelle, Sarah, and myself burst through the foliage partially blocking our exit from the alleyway, to come upon a scene of sun, sea, and sand. There were a few people lying around on wooden sun beds. They didn't have to walk far--their accommodation opened directly out onto the beach. One of the men spoke to me, saying there were stones in the water; it was much better further on (so what was he doing here then?). The man sounded German (and was holding a can that said 'Heinz') prompting the thought that maybe he didn't want us to spoil their occupation of this area (they did occupy a few areas over the duration of two world wars). But to be fair, I knew already Rockley, and further up, St. James, were good locations.

When I ventured into the water, treacherous stones and rocks lay scattered about under my feet--Karl Heinz Fritz was right then. The water came up to my waist here, any further out and the seabed was all rocks. Where Michelle and I stood now was bad enough and probably a bit too dangerous for swimming, though it felt nice going into the water for the first time--however carefully we had to tread. Dawn, who came to meet us not long after we had left the apartment, stood watching nearby with Sarah.

It was at this point that a moment of Caribbean theatre was about to unfold. As soon as Michelle and myself were on the beach again, a black Bajan man sporting long dreadlocks and matching tattered shorts (reminding me of Bob Marley--when he wore tattered shorts), came walking towards us. In his hand was a piece of green plant, which looked like jelly on one side. The 'Rasta man' said:

"You have to watch out for the sun" (you don't say...)

"This plant is good for protecting the skin and its natural man"

Its name was 'Aloe Vera'.

All the time while he's talking, he's not asking for anything, just being friendly. Then, after putting some of the stuff on us, the Bajan man tells me I can have a little; he'll put it in a bottle for only B20--why thanks man, that's only £6 you're asking me for some sticky jelly off a plant, wow, great deal. I tell him this is expensive.

"Oh" he says: "This plant cost over a hundred dollars to buy" (yeah, right...)

But okay, he'll give it to me for B10--to which I agree. It's not often I can strike myself some sort of bargain. The Rasta makes more conversation--like 'where do I come from?' (That's easy--banana boat)

"Oh, my middle names Mark as well, hey I've got a family too" (you don't say...).

Then our friend gets out a long leaf of green cactus like plant, which he cuts open, at the same time

Chapter 4: Aloe Vera

producing an old, empty, and half litre rum bottle. With his knife, the Bajan man starts scooping out the jelly from the inside of the plant, pushing it into the small bottle, spilling some over the sides. This all being done with an expertise, suggesting he had been paid for bottles of plant jelly many times before. Our Rasta friend only half filled it, and I said to him:

"There's only half a bottle there"

He replied: "Oh Mark, you're robbing me" (I'm robbing him...?).

Then he produced another piece of plant, and scooped out a bit of jelly into the bottle--again spilling some over the sides. The Bajan Rasta told me you had to add a little water every three days, and the jelly will grow back (what is this--Quatermass?). The only surprise left now, was that the price had risen from B10 to B15--and he says I'm robbing him! This beach hyena was having the last laugh, picking the bones of my wallet clean.

The Rasta walked off up the sandy shore. He looked as if he had nothing, but he had a bit of old cactus plant and my B15. I had the jelly and a lighter wallet. I stood briefly staring after him, wondering if I had been well and truly doped. An innocent abroad was fair game for a Bajan hustler. This was the last time I listened to anybody who was trying to sell me something; from now on we would just say no and not enter into any conversation--I said to Dawn determinedly. Dawn, who had been standing only a few feet away during my purchase of the jelly, looked with an unsurprised face at me and the bottle, then remarked in a voice tinged with boredom:

"I told you just say no, didn't I--don't talk to them"

Dawn thought I always talked too much whenever these people began bothering me. We went to the same school, but had both learned something entirely different. I was a green lemon on the beach, whereas Dawn could maneuver through this minefield of slick talking beggar entrepreneurs, like the young George Best against a Bournemouth old folks home second eleven. Ironically, as it turned out--the stuff was pretty good.

Brushing most of the sand off my feet, I put my socks and shoes on and carried Sarah back under one arm, with her feet still sandy. At the apartment, I got a large plastic beaker filled with water, then out on the porch, washed the sand off Sarah and Michelle's feet before they could go inside for their showers. We had bought a big sweet potato in Bridgetown and frozen peas in the little shop around the corner. I fell asleep about 19:00hr, as Dawn was preparing the dinner. No doubt I was dreaming of life without Aloe Vera. The potato needed peeling, and it wasn't that easy to do (I know because I had the first go).

Opening my eyes a few hours later, I found everybody asleep, with Sarah beside me. I went into the kitchen, discovering that dinner had been cooked, after a fashion. The sweet potato looking black in places, but not tasting too bad--though there was no

Chapter 4: Aloe Vera

salt. The peas were delicious. Afterwards I sat in the lounge, writing up my diary as the odd mosquito buzzed and hid out of sight. Ants could be seen occasionally on the furniture, sometimes on the floor. Presently, Dawn, Michelle, and Sarah woke up also and we talked about our stay here so far and our plans for tomorrow. I suggested visiting the Zoo--having earlier looked through a handful of pamphlets, taken from the airport. It meant travelling to Bridgetown and then catching a bus. Not long into this discussion, Dawn, Michelle, and Sarah dozed off; at 02:00hr--so did I.

Chapter 5

A DAY AT THE ZOO

In the morning, I was up first, washing a few socks and things. I cooked Michelle and Sarah eggs for breakfast. Michelle and Dawn like toast, though Dawn always has a bowl of cornflakes to start with. Sarah eats in bits and pieces, exactly like Mercy; having a biscuit now and again; drinking mostly water like her mum. Dawn and I have to change more traveller's cheques at the bank today. It's only a few yards away, so that shouldn't be a problem.

Later, while in the bank, I am told that our little shop--'99 convenience store' as it's called--sells stamps and there are post boxes nearby. Unfortunately for us, the stamps are not for the UK; now we'll have to find the post office in Bridgetown to send our postcards home, before travelling on to the zoo.

Passing the taxis, their drivers lurking, crouching in anticipation--ready to pounce on any tourist who dares to use their legs for a while--we head towards the main road and buses to Bridgetown. On the way, I look inside a shop mostly filled with t-shirts. There was one like Michelle's killer whale shirt, but this was of humpback whales. Although tempted, I decided not to buy. Dawn had bought her hat from this shop the other day.

At a little wooden kiosk daubed 'Information Centre' (but looking more like Mrs. Robinson's display of gardening leaflets at a summer fete), a Bajan woman asked me if I wanted to go for a free lunch, apparently involving timeshare. A free lunch is wonderful anytime, but timeshare? This woman had also stopped us the day before, but told me then we had to be husband and wife--so why ask me again? (Probably a relative of the old lady, small island you know). Our new rule which said 'no' to anybody suggesting we do something they ask us, was now fully in effect; and after learning from her that there was a short cut to the main road, we went on our way. The short cut took us through a pleasant tree lined area with apartments either side.

Soon after reaching the main road, I hailed a mini-bus and with the rhythm of the beat pounding in our ears, we flew down the tarmac. On the way, I saw a big cruise liner in the dock, filled no doubt to the brim with happy holiday makers. It must have cost them a fortune (unlike my little visit, which came complete with free flights for myself and the children--the pain in the neck being accommodation costs and spending money).

Before long our mini-bus arrived at the parking area on the edge of Bridgetown. As we walked towards the town, I tried to borrow Dawn's hat and then asked an old man for directions to the post office. The old man pointed the way, telling me to go down Broad Street (wherever that was). I marched on, expecting to find it soon, keeping in the shade as much as possible. Standing in the open was like getting your face too close to an oven. Every now and then I asked someone again where the post office was. It seemed we were walking right across Bridgetown, and there still remained our main objective--a visit to the zoo.

Stopping at a place called 'The Jubilee Bus Station', which was smaller than the main one, the four of us par-took of some liquid refreshment. The time and distance involved in sending post cards was becoming irritating--not to mention laborious. Minutes later, just past the bus station, we finally arrived at what Dawn said must be the post office--after walking all the way across Bridgetown to get to it.

Post office? This building was more like something out of the old Fritz Lang film Metropolis to me. A sort of stone, monolithic monstrosity, with a big light bulb and rows of aimless steps leading everywhere. There were some odd direction signs and a long glass section, which somehow looked as if it might be for public use. Inside was more space than anybody needed (you wouldn't use Earls Court as a

Chapter 5: A Day at the Zoo

local post office).

We queued up, bought the stamps at 70 cents each, and discovered they were the same as those on sale in the ever popular '99 Convenience Store' in St. Lawrence Gap. I stuck them on the post cards, pleased this escapade was over. Dawn said in her wise and sagely manner, that anyway, the post office would be the quickest way to send them home (this made me feel much better--after all we'd been through--knowing they would probably get back a day or so sooner). Managing only a thin smile, I wished we had simply put the letters in the box outside the 99 store.

Tweedle-Dum, Tweedle-Dee, their auntie, and the Cheshire Cat began walking back to the mini-bus station. A mini-bus conductor (who was in fact a normal size man) showed us to his vehicle--he would be taking a route which included Oughton Zoo, I was assured. It turned out that this mini-bus was travelling right over to the other side of the island first, before passing somewhere near the zoo on the way back. Looking on the positive side, I got to see varied and interesting scenery whilst travelling the width of Barbados, with the added bonus of a panoramic view of the far-side coastline.

During this tour--which hadn't cost me a penny more than the basic bus fare--I began to puzzle as to the whereabouts of aforementioned zoo. I was not alone in this lack of knowledge, for our man behind the steering wheel didn't seem to have a clue either, needing to ask directions from anyone he could find as we left the seascape behind us. It wasn't far though--nothing on Barbados is all that far because the island is so small--and when the driver came upon a sign proclaiming 'Zoo Oughton House', even he realized this must be the place; and after dropping us off, quickly sped away in embarrassment (no doubt without knowing in which direction he was going).

It seemed we were right out in the middle of nowhere (and we were really), with a long, high grassed verged, leafy lane to walk down before reaching the zoo. In a short while, the gates of Oughton House became visible. I paid a little, very dark skinned, crinkly faced old lady the entrance money, picked up a zoo map and the four of us ventured in.

It was only a small place, nothing too grand or high and mighty. On our left a hundred yards away, was Oughton House itself--an old plantation house from the 1700's. Just inside the front doorway stood an elderly white man, his clothes and general appearance harkening back to those old days of plantation slavery. He welcomed us as we walked through the door, and introduced his parrots to the children. On the walls on one side of this first part of the house, there were t-shirts and gift items hanging up--contrasting with the historical atmosphere of the building. The parrots were quite funny, saying (amongst other things):

"Hello Joey" (a standard line for parrots of course, even if your name wasn't Joey. Parrots are very clever; to make their life easier they just give everyone the same name). When they laughed it made us laugh too.

I asked the man why there were so many front doors and open linked rooms (these were joined by archways that had French doors, if you wanted to close the rooms off from each other). Our host replied the reason was with this design you could cool the house by having a breeze blowing all the way through. Useful in what must have been (and still are) many a sweat laden day. Noticing the worn tiled flooring here at the front of the house, I wondered whether it went back to the old plantation days. The elderly man said it did, before mentioning that this plantation was relatively small, being only a hundred and fifty acres.

Going into the middle rooms, we saw some very solid antique furniture that was, we were told, real Bajan mahogany. The furniture was original and indigenous--being about the only thing that was not imported in those days. A number of crocodile (or alligator?) skins were draped over some of the handsome mahogany sideboards. The man, who seemed to be part of that history himself, said the back half of the house was more recent, dating from around the 1870's or thereabouts--still a long time ago I thought. A couple of black maids dusted and swept the floor, as if the balance of power had never altered in hundreds of years.

At the back of the house, we entered the first part of the zoo; a sort of conservatory where there were fish and snakes in glass tanks. The two biggest fish--with a frightening array of sharp teeth--looked like piranhas to me (after all, how many other fish have teeth--let alone teeth like that); a boy employed at the house said they were. He also said the piranhas would grow to five or six pounds, although to my magnifying glass eyes (at this moment) these fish looked plenty big enough already.

Coming out from the back of the house into the sun again, we suddenly became surrounded by monkeys and parrots. One of the monkeys acted a bit mad with us--for whatever reason--and another banana chomper, Dawn oddly thought was a cross between a monkey and a rabbit because it looked like there was a white rabbit in the cage with it. Somehow I didn't think this was Doom Watch (a seventies science fiction series) revisited, with experiments in genetics--more a case of Dawn's fanciful imagination breaking loose (Alice in Wonderland chasing the White Rabbit with a pocket watch).

Dawn commented that it was wrong--these monkeys and birds kept in cages. I replied I suppose it was, as they haven't got enough room; your life restricted to bouncing around in a pokey cage, decorated with a few branches, half a tree, and an old rubber tire to swing on if you get bored (which I'm sure they must have done occasionally--not having a television). Yes, I don't suppose it is right really. No wonder they get mad with people looking at them:

"Why are you out there, while I'm in here?" he's saying (and if you met some of the people I know, you'd realize there wasn't really an answer to that)

Chapter 5: A Day at the Zoo

The parrots next to the monkey cages were making a lot of noise--maybe they thought Long John Silver was coming back for them.

We walked along the path and approached another cage. Inside were some large parrots, displaying an abundance of tropical colour. These birds were a bit more upmarket, not noisy; unlike the other ugly type of parrot, who had to find a way of getting people to look at them, hence all the histrionics. In the last bird cage, across the yard, fairly on its own, was the domain of a few beautiful big brown owls. A mouse scampered around just inside the cage, as the owls watched with large brown eyes--so intelligently I felt they might speak to us at any moment.

Going down steps, towards a zebra pen, we found ourselves in a small fenced area where tortoises were roaming. Sarah loved it, she got down to talk to them and tried picking one up. I told her it was best not to because if she dropped the tortoise it might die. On one side, through a little gate, there were two crocodile pens. These lads were only about four feet long, but the look on their faces was very evil, a more malevolent face you would not expect to find (maybe not here, but I could think of a few back home).

I decided to walk back up the steps because directly across the yard was a small cage that seemed to have something interesting in it. They were mongooses, but as we approached, the weasel looking animals quickly hid inside their house; so we walked past them, through a shed with guinea pigs on a shelf, and came out the other side. On our right were a couple of pens containing Tapirs. I mentioned that they were funny looking things, Michelle though, commented on these animals being half like a hog and half like an anteater, which was a much more intelligent observation. A coloured lady (no doubt Bajan) standing alongside us said:

"She's right you know."

Yes, yes, yes, I know she's right--why does she have to poke her anteater sized nose in? I wondered why Tapirs had to have a nose that was like the last eight inches of an elephant's trunk. Maybe it's because they're nosey parkers like the Bajan woman standing beside us, otherwise I can't see an advantage--except to join the noisy parrots' ugly club.

Going back past the zebras, we saw a few goats and another animal, which took us to the end of the zoo trail. Although not very big, the zoo had been interesting. Now spotting the refreshment counter, Dawn, Michelle, and Sarah wanted to sit down. The adjoining restroom was surprisingly clean, a commendable standard indeed. Dawn agreed, taking the opportunity to once more carry the torch and express her admiration for the cleanliness of Bajan toilets (which is all very well, as long as you're not the one who has to clean them). How much of this advanced civilization is due to the Englishman we met earlier is uncertain, but I would guess that these hygienic facilities are mostly through his efforts--enslaving Bajans to constantly maintain the standard.

Chapter 5: A Day at the Zoo

We relaxed, shaded from the sun. Sarah had ice cream, Michelle and Dawn dived into a plate of chips each, splattered with vinegar, salt, and tomato ketchup. I didn't have anything, but then accepted a few chips when offered them. After we had gone, Dawn said the chips were horrible--though I fail to see how she could have tasted the food under all that condiment. Anyway she ate the lot, so they couldn't have been all that bad.

Soon it was time to leave if we were to make St. Lawrence before nightfall. I didn't want us to be stuck anywhere--especially leafy, long grassed, jungle like areas veritably out in the sticks--when it began to get dark. We trekked up to the road, where the bus had dropped us. As I reached the stop, wouldn't you know it, one went past. A few minutes later, there was another bus approaching. Dawn declared in a droll sort of voice, that it was a visitor's bus, not the one we wanted--so I didn't stick my arm out. But after it had gone by and left us in its wake, Dawn said I should have because it probably was for us. I had time to think about this, as there was supposed to be a bus every hour. It could be a very long wait, and with the sun's rays still hot, I was at least grateful to Dawn for letting me borrow her hat occasionally.

I certainly wasn't going to blame anyone in particular, that would be unfair; so I didn't say it was Dawn's fault that here we were, barely able to stand up on aching, rubbery legs, after a grueling day in the tormenting Barbados sun; waiting patiently for a public bus whilst our bodies' melted slowly into the soft Bajan tarmac. Furthermore, the prospect of seeing the sun set over the hills of Barbados through red veined weary eyes; and still being in this wilderness immediately surrounding us--was becoming a very real, unappetizing possibility. Sarah wanted me to carry her. No one ever carried me when I got tired.

Luckily for those of us that were stranded, it wasn't long before a saviour arrived. Our feet were on the bus before you could say 'Jack Robinson' (somehow finding renewed energy), and as we settled down in the seats, there was an audible collective sigh of relief.

Later on, while on the second bus back to St. Lawrence, Michelle noticed we had gone past the place we wanted to get off, on the main road, before walking back down to St. Lawrence Gap. I couldn't understand it; after all, I had my eyes open too--didn't I? As well as being stupid, mean, selfish, inconsiderate, sometimes tight (though, to be fair, that's debatable), and lacking in commonsense--did I need glasses? Being only seventy-five percent sure, I led the way down the winding road that took us back to our apartment, as the night-life of St. Lawrence sprang up all around.

While Michelle, Sarah, and myself settled on the beds for a rest, Dawn cooked the remaining potatoes. Dawn and I had decided to move on to another part of the island tomorrow, more than likely in St. James if possible, where I believed the beaches and swimming would be better. Part of our plan involved slipping away stealthily and silently, without coming into contact with the old lady--because we suspected she might charge us extra for the air-conditioning.

Chapter 6

FLIGHT OF THE NAVIGATORS

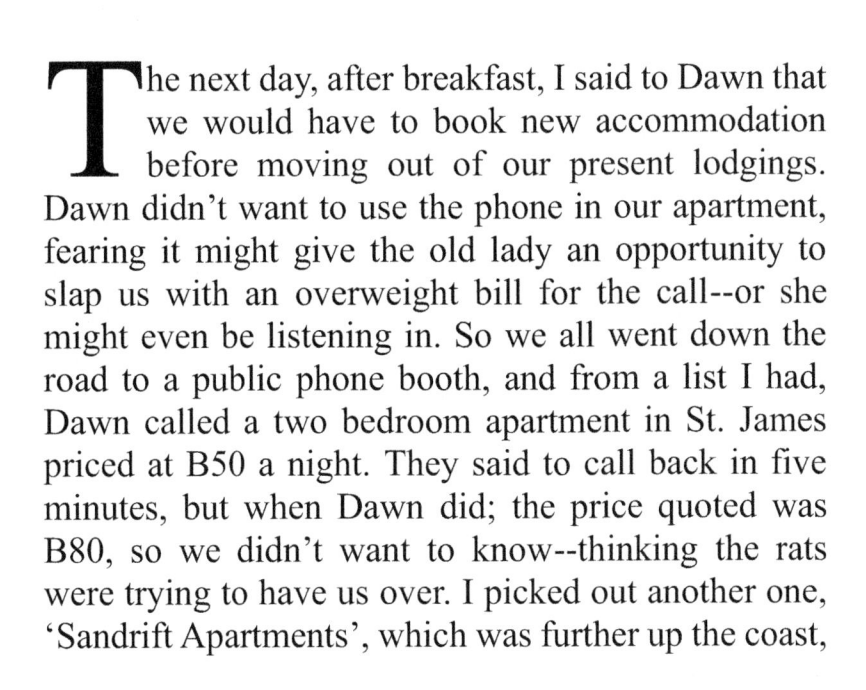

The next day, after breakfast, I said to Dawn that we would have to book new accommodation before moving out of our present lodgings. Dawn didn't want to use the phone in our apartment, fearing it might give the old lady an opportunity to slap us with an overweight bill for the call--or she might even be listening in. So we all went down the road to a public phone booth, and from a list I had, Dawn called a two bedroom apartment in St. James priced at B50 a night. They said to call back in five minutes, but when Dawn did; the price quoted was B80, so we didn't want to know--thinking the rats were trying to have us over. I picked out another one, 'Sandrift Apartments', which was further up the coast,

Chapter 6: Flight of the Navigators

just before St. James. Dawn said that there was only a one bedroom apartment available, but they could put a third bed in the room if we wanted it (at no extra cost), and the room was quite big, the lady said. Dawn listened to directions over the phone on how to find Sandrift, and then told me she liked the way this woman sounded, and had a good feeling about our decision to go there. It was 11:50hr now; we had to check out at midday.

Back at the apartment, Dawn, Michelle, Sarah, and myself brought all the luggage outside onto the porch, and I snapped the big padlock shut on the door--ready for the next lucky people to check in. Who knows, it could well be some of those good friends who keep in touch with old Madame Money Grabber. One thing for sure, there wouldn't be a letter on her wall from us in the future, saying how looking forward we were to coming back.

I was going to ask Michelle to drop the keys off, hoping this maneuver would conveniently allow Dawn and me to avoid crossing paths with our host; she might pull one last trick on us, to get me to put my hand in my pocket. But I liked my wallet the way it was, hermetically sealed with a cellophane wrapping and tucked deep into the bottom of my specially made pockets; that went so far down--I could scratch my knees without taking my hands out.

Dawn argued that sending Michelle wouldn't be right, one of us should go--but it wasn't going to be her. So I volunteered, being the third bravest after Sarah and Michelle. Fortunately, the maid was alone in the house, and sucking in a sigh of relief, I handed over the keys. The maid smiled as she wished us a good holiday and I said goodbye.

Somehow you can always recognize another Englishman when you're abroad. I saw one across the road as we vacated the apartment. I asked him if there was a shorter route to the main road, other than the one I already knew of, which took us past the taxis and through the town (the vultures were sure to pester us if we walked by carrying all our luggage). The man said, if we took the opposite direction and followed the road to the left, it wasn't far.

Setting off, carrying the two heaviest pieces of luggage (in Barbados), one mine and the other Dawn's, I was happy enough knowing we were saving £4 on the trip to Bridgetown by this method. From Bridgetown we could catch a bus to our new accommodation. It was simple; all we had to do was get going. As I rounded the bend a little further up, lounging on the left was a posse of taxi drivers; but they might as well have been taxidermists for all the business they'd be getting from us. On the right hand side was the 'Casurina Beach Club', which had been highly recommended to me by comrades at work. The taxis were obviously waiting to pick the bones of the first wallet (for this is all they see when they look at a tourist) that came out through those gilded gates.

It was a bit of a slog for me with the heavy bags, but when Dawn complained loudly of the sufferings she was enduring on this little walk of ours, I couldn't believe my ears. Dawn only had fairly light luggage to

Chapter 6: Flight of the Navigators

carry--you'd think it was a cooker and sofa bed. But to be fair, I suppose Dawn still wasn't feeling all that well. Another matter dividing our attention was Sarah wandering out from the roadside, which could be hazardous because the roads were too narrow and the traffic quite busy. Come to think of it, there are very few paths in Barbados--probably to force the tourists to take a taxi. I bet the Bajan government siphon off a healthy percentage of their profit.

In half an hour we had reached the main road and a bus stop. Dawn was surprised that it did appear to be a shorter route. I could sit down now for a moment and afford a smile, while at the same time wondering when my newly stretched arms would return to their original length and the bones fit comfortably back into their sockets. The only advantage I can see in having four foot arms is that I might find it easier to reach my wallet.

Suddenly, someone in a mini-bus travelling in the opposite direction for Bridgetown called out asking if we were going to Bridgetown--I said:

"Yes, but not that way"

The driver promptly turned around in the middle of the road to pick us up. There were no other passengers, they were just looking for a fare and didn't mind going back where they had come from. Pulsing, youngsters' hip-hop music entertained our ears as we flew along the road. This time, coming near to Bridgetown, I didn't see a ship in dock.

When the mini-bus arrived at the car-park, somebody asked us where we were going. I told him the Black Rock bus shelter near the Paradise Hotel. Apparently that's where he was going, so the four of us went with him to a mini-bus a few yards away. I asked how much for the fare, and getting no reply assumed it would be about B6--like any other mini-bus. We were their only passengers and in less than twenty minutes or so, the driver stopped outside an Esso petrol station, which he said was near the Paradise Beach Club.

Dawn took a picture of Michelle, Sarah, and myself standing in front of the mini-bus with two of the three Bajans who had accompanied us on the bus. The third one, having returned from a quick visit to the Esso station, then explained that this was a private job which costs more than normal--it would be B15. Of course, doing these sorts of jobs in groups of threes gave them a distinct advantage if the passengers disagreed with their underhand business tactics and looked to cause trouble. They deserved a good slapping from four or five gorillas in the mist, but Dawn and I had to put this down to experience, so, frowning, I coughed up. As these 'tricky dickeys' sped away, Dawn jokingly said we could report them, as their faces and the mini-bus registration would be on the photograph (A good idea--but I preferred the gorillas). What Dawn and I didn't like, was not being told it would cost more to start with. Dawn never wanted to use the mini-buses again after this, and we never did, choosing from then on to stick loyally to the two types of larger buses, which were more trustworthy in all respects. I believe these buses were government funded and therefore not profit motivated. For the others--the only correct solution is to enlist a few silverbacks.

Dawn asked a woman for directions, and was told something about getting on a bus to Speight town. We climbed aboard one and went a mile further up the coastal road, before finding out from people travelling with us, that the stop outside the Esso station was the Black Rock bus shelter I was looking for. I got angry because I thought the bus conductor had turned me over, but he didn't charge for the ride (which made me feel much better) and we soon caught another bus back to our original point.

Leaving the Esso station behind, the four of us walked a little way up to a roundabout, then a few hundred yards past that, turned right into a small road which led round a bend on the left, and subsequently, steeply downwards to the right, between blocks of attractive apartments. I asked directions from someone, who helpfully pointed out the place we were looking for--another fifty yards downhill on the right hand side. This looked more like an upmarket area, close to the sea as well. Dawn and I were impressed by the smart, clean, three story building; surely the Sandrift Apartments would be just as good inside.

Chapter 7

SANDRIFT

I walked around the front and through the door marked 'office'. There was a small, fairly young black woman behind the counter. Her manner was friendly and helpful. We were to find her open and honest in her dealings with us. The manageress told me the price was inclusive and that she would install a third bed which normally they'd charge for. Dawn and I were pleased with the favourable arrangements; also with the apartment itself. There was a large lounge with a kitchenette at one end--even a toaster, kettle and coffee percolator supplied. The walls were constructed from big blocks of concrete finished in a clean white, and the floors--shining as if new--made up of large, square white tiles, flecked with black. Leading off the lounge, opposite the front door, was the outside balcony--a neat, square area with a roof and red tiled floor. Around the two open sides of the balcony were two and a half foot black metal railings; a table and two chairs were provided for our relaxation. The view from here was almost completely filled by trees, that all stood higher than the block of apartments itself.

The bedroom was quite big, as the lady had said--enough for a third bed without introducing a claustrophobic atmosphere. We had ample wardrobe space with three sliding doors and numerous drawers. Between the two wardrobes was a large vanity mirror with light, and underneath, a table top and drawers. The very clean bathroom additionally boasted an impressive looking shower. The lounge and bedroom windows were fitted with wooden shutters, designed to be open during the day and closed at night, in an effort to keep out mosquitoes. Our bedroom was also equipped with the luxury of an air-conditioning unit.

Separating the kitchenette from the lounge was a square archway, made from wrought iron in the design of an entwining creeper. The chairs, tables and light stands were fashioned in wrought iron along the same theme, to complement the archway. All this internal iron work was finished in white paint.

Our host told us the Sandrift Apartments were built over thirty years ago. When Dawn and I thought about this later in the day--after we had been swimming--we realized most of the furniture and fittings were in fact originals: Lounge table with glass top, chairs, coffee table--glass top again, settee, tall light stand, table light, bedroom units and drawers, vanity mirror seat, bedside table light, hand held shower. In the kitchenette; the cupboards, drawers, cooker, kettle, teapot, sink and taps, coffee percolator--all looked 1960's era, except for the fridge freezer unit. Our guess was that these apartments were probably used by affluent people during the swinging sixties--when this accommodation would have been the height of luxury. Even in these days it didn't seem too bad either. I enjoyed the idea of staying in an authentic sixties apartment. Of course, our own mother still uses one or two items that are thirty years old or more; but here nearly everything had acquired antique status.

After settling in and storing away the luggage, we got changed for the beach. The manageress told us that at the bottom of the road, there were some gates to what used to be the old Paradise Village Hotel, which was now closed. It was possible to go around those gates, through a gap at the side, our host said; walking through the old hotel grounds would be the quickest way to the beach.

A little while later, Dawn, myself, Michelle, and Sarah--resplendent in beach clothes--passed around the gate, finding ourselves on premises that had not been attended to for a very long time; there was a lot of moss and grass growing up through the paths. The days of splendour had long since passed here, leaving only patchy reminders of the better times. Coming out the other side, we jumped down a foot or two onto the sand. There was the Barbados Sea once again.

On the south coast, in St Lawrence, the sea had surf, waves, but here on the western side, it was much

Chapter 7: Sandrift

calmer and the water also seemed to get deep very quickly. Sarah would only stay in when Dawn or I carried her. Land, sea, or air--Sarah still wants to be carried. The beach is a little untidy because the big hotels on the front here have been closed awhile; as a result there are not enough tourists to make it worthwhile doing a regular clear up. We enjoy ourselves in the water; it's a long time since I've been in the sea. The beach line stretches up to a corner which I'm curious about as to what lies around the bend. Maybe another day we'll explore further, for now we've had a nice dip and it's time to go back for a shower and something to eat.

As we walk up the steep road to our apartment, Dawn says to me that there is a sign outside the Sandrift building boasting they have the largest rooms on the island. The old lady in 'Four Aces' said the same thing, but as I told Dawn--in her case it was probably the biggest liar on the island. We both laughed at this.

Later, after showering and changing, all of us went out to a little local mini-mart (supermarket); which as you come out at the top of our little road, was just across the main road and to the right. Our host said this would be cheaper (a big consideration for me) than the mini-mart at the Esso station. There wasn't any air-conditioning in the shop, no fresh vegetables either, and as we slowly walked around, a big Bajan man loomed over me while I stopped to examine a box of refrigerated beers. He asked me if I liked banks; about five minutes later, after he'd asked me another twenty times, I realized it was the name of the local beer. I said yes and bought two. This man was wide, blocking the isles, so that anywhere we were in the shop--he seemed to be in the way. There was hardly any room to start with, and then Dawn wasn't very happy because she said he kept leaning over her all the time.

We came out the shop with some rice, peas, beer, soft drinks, bread, margarine, and tuna. None of us went there again. From then on, any local shopping was done at the Esso garage, with its great air-conditioning, tasty donuts, plentiful choice of products, ample space to move around, and no giant Bajan natives looming over you--even if they are friendly.

Dawn cooked rice that night. It didn't come out right, she said only because basically there was too much water (the birds ended up eating most of her rice the next morning). Dawn was though, to cook us some nice dinners over the next few days. While we were waiting for dinner, Dawn said:

"Fridge's open again"

I said:

"It doesn't open by itself, does it--Michelle, did you leave the fridge open?"

Michelle then replied in a matter of fact voice:

"The fridge doesn't open by itself, what was the other question you asked me daddy?"

Chapter 7: Sandrift

  I washed up. On our hectic journey to get here, I had brought the remaining eggs from our stay at 'Four Aces'. Dawn wasn't impressed when I told her they were in one of the bags I'd been lugging around all day. That night turned out to be the best sleep we'd had up till then.

                Z

             Z

        Z

In snooze mode we soundly slept
While outside, the angels an eye on us kept

              Z

           Z

        Z

When darkness had vanished, and daylight begun
It was time to rise up, and go out in the sun.

Chapter 8

AROUND THE BEND

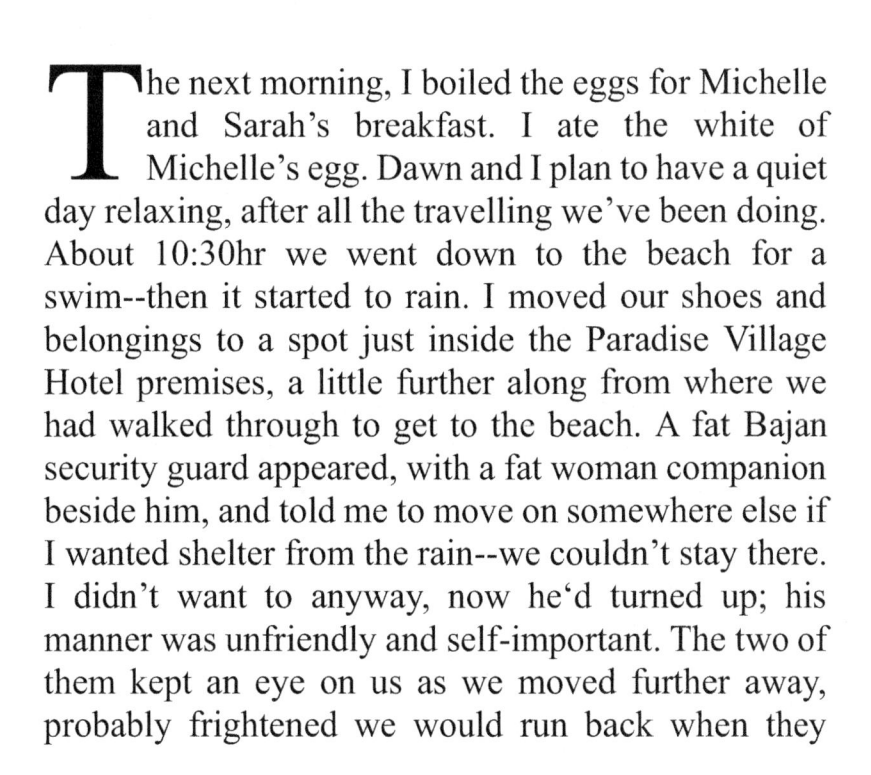

The next morning, I boiled the eggs for Michelle and Sarah's breakfast. I ate the white of Michelle's egg. Dawn and I plan to have a quiet day relaxing, after all the travelling we've been doing. About 10:30hr we went down to the beach for a swim--then it started to rain. I moved our shoes and belongings to a spot just inside the Paradise Village Hotel premises, a little further along from where we had walked through to get to the beach. A fat Bajan security guard appeared, with a fat woman companion beside him, and told me to move on somewhere else if I wanted shelter from the rain--we couldn't stay there. I didn't want to anyway, now he'd turned up; his manner was unfriendly and self-important. The two of them kept an eye on us as we moved further away, probably frightened we would run back when they

Chapter 8: Around the Bend

weren't looking, and trespass on their master's territory. These blights on an otherwise pleasant landscape, had nothing else to do all day I suppose but bark at decent people trying to have a holiday.

It was still raining, and Dawn said she didn't want to catch a cold, as she's just had one thank you very much. Dawn decided to go back to the apartment, while I stayed in the sea with the children. It looked like a wet day at Ruislip Lido, but what could you do? The rainy season was supposed to be over, yet we'd just managed to catch the last gasp of it.

Not much later, Michelle, Sarah, and myself walk back in Dawn's footsteps, and it's not very comfortable when we go up the steep road in bare feet because of all the little stones. The time is 12:30hr, and we're having a break until later on in the afternoon when I plan to take them to the beach again.

We are in the rooms relaxing when Michelle says that the birds are eating cheese on our balcony. Dawn and I said:

"Don't be silly, they won't eat cheese..."

But Michelle said they did and put a couple of pieces on the rail. Soon, low and behold, a little brown bird began sampling the cheese. I said:

"Dawn, the bird's eating the cheese, they've got cheese eating birds here..."

Michelle then pointed out in a matter of fact tone:

"Silly, they're birds eating cheese, not cheese eating birds…"

We are about to leave for the beach again. The others are pushing to go right away, but I must get some of Dawn's sunblock on first or my nose will burn. Dawn says we have to leave before it gets dark (she must be like dad). Dawn's plastered in white sunblock, some of it in her hair. I can see Michelle in the bedroom painting her nails. I exclaim incredulously to Dawn what Michelle is doing. Dawn says I make it sound like she robbed a bank. Michelle says its only nail strengthener. Looks like a mongoose outside, near our apartment.

At about three o'clock in the afternoon, the four of us made our way down to the beach. I said to Dawn, that this time we could walk up to the bend and see what's round the other side. On the bend there are a lot of large flat rocks that the sea just washes over. Not many shells around here, but Michelle has picked up some small ones. I walk on further, and turning the corner discover what appears to be a favourite swimming spot for the local people. There are some wooden tables and benches under the shade of a few tall trees. A couple of days later, when we passed this way again, there were a lot of young people here; but for the moment it remained a place of quiet remoteness, only briefly interrupted by our presence.

Nearby two Bajan men were fishing off a rock, using hand held lines. Wearing only shorts, their dark bodies stood out starkly against a panoramic background of endless blue water. They went about

Chapter 8: Around the Bend

their toil as if nothing had changed in thirty years. The vast and mysterious sea that stretched out behind them had never changed, it was timeless... Ahead, the beach stopped under the shade of a short rock cliff that continued on around another bend. Our little excursion had led us to a dead end. On top of the cliff were some houses, and a tiny figure moved slowly in one of the gardens high above.

We lay our belongings down on the beach about fifty yards from the cliff side and waded into the warm, clear water. Dawn and I thought it was a perfectly lovely spot to go swimming in the sea. Instead of sharp rocks strewn in unknown places, our feet felt only the comfort of a soft, sandy seabed. I carried Sarah into the water with me, and then looked back at the beach. A hundred yards or so from the water's edge, masses of thickly foliaged trees reached high into the cloudless blue sky. In this paradise we basked in the glory of nature.

At one point, a bajan man called out to us from the beach. He looked very much like the person who had shouted to me earlier in the day--when I was on the balcony of our hotel room--asking if I wanted freshly caught fish. It sounded as if he asked 'was I somebody or other', and I just replied:

"No"

The incident unsettled Dawn and myself slightly, after all, this was a quiet, secluded area. But of course, there are a lot of these ragamuffin beach people about, who pop up without warning every now and again--like smiling, little brown jack in the boxes. Fortunately, every time Dawn and I have told them we don't want to know, that has been the end of it. Despite this comforting piece of knowledge, I still found myself looking expectantly into the trees once in a while, but nobody--nor jack in the box--appeared, and at 1700hrs the four of us made our way back to the apartment.

Michelle cooked rice that night, with peas; we're not doing so badly. Sometimes in the evenings, Michelle and Sarah have these silly moments. Michelle's gravitate towards premeditated aggravation; Sarah's are more as a result of bounding around with joy. I fell asleep about eight or nine, while hearing what sounded like three different voices talking at the same time. It was Dawn, Michelle, and Sarah playing charades. I guess it wouldn't be much longer before they too enjoyed the comfort of a good night's sleep.

Chapter 9

THE FLOWER FOREST

I'm up early this morning. Its 0600hr, and our sixth day in Barbados. As dad is fond of saying, 'If you sleep late, half the day is gone'. I sit outside on the balcony to write my diary. The others won't get up yet, so I'll have some solitude for a while. I put some rice out for the birds. Three come straight away; a big brown one like a pigeon, and two little brown ones. The other birds we have seen are black. Of course the living world around us is always up at this time--almost without exception (Dawn and bats being exceptions).

I've just seen the manageress downstairs wearing a red towel on her head and a red towel wrapped around her. She had come out to throw something down and go back in. The manageress

Chapter 9: The Flower Forest

looked up and said good morning. I only waved back, maybe I should have said hello. The sun is lighting up the tops of the trees next to me, butterflies flying around them. That big pigeon looking bird has eaten all the rice I put down. Funny looking things birds, their heads jerking about all the time. I can see two mongooses where our host threw something earlier. Maybe that's what she was doing, putting some food out for them. I'll have to ask her if they are mongooses. Really it's a bit of an aviary we've got next to us with all these birds.

I've been up for an hour and a half now, its 0725hr and I haven't seen the others yet. Dawn and I plan to go to the Flower Forest today using the buses. This means going to Bridgetown first, then catching another bus from the Jubilee Station at the post office end of town. It's not the shortest route to take, but we're trying to get about more cheaply, and the low exchange rate makes taxis an expensive option. Eventually Sarah gets up, followed by Michelle, and lastly, with a great deal of effort--so does Dawn.

We have our breakfast at the glass table in the lounge, and thereafter, slowly get ready for today's adventure. It is almost midday by the time everyone is on the starting line. Dawn and myself apply a modicum of her sun cream to our visages. Michelle and Sarah do not need any protection from the sun, they just go brown. After our usual short walk--which always seems longer due to the heat--we wait at the bus stop opposite the Esso station, going back in the direction of Bridgetown.

On arriving at the Jubilee Station, we then had to stand around for quite a long while. Our host at Sandrift had told Dawn and I that the buses going to Shorey 'something' and the Lakes would take us to the Flower Forest, but at the moment there were none of those here. The Jubilee Station was really a small, hundred square yard bus park, with signs for the destinations located at stops punctuated equally around the sides. When a bus came in, it reversed up to the stops, so facing the center of the park ready to leave. There was one small enclosed bus shelter, and a little garden shed sized refreshment shop. The only shade I could find was at the back of the wooden shed.

I watched the bustling life of Bridgetown pass us by, first standing, then sitting on a piece of concrete, contemplating the thoughts of Aristotle; the origins of the universe; the Great Pyramid at Giza; why we're having to wait so long for a bus, before standing up again. Finally our transport arrived--Flower Forest here we come. As everybody tried to get on the bus, I noticed some young people--who had only just turned up at the last minute--trying to squeeze in to the front. There wasn't an orderly queue, but I said to one of them:

"You were well behind us"

It's one off the things I don't like. I'm quite prepared to take my turn when it comes, and I expect others to play fair as well. When I made my indignant remark, from the back of a surge of people jostling to get on from another angle--to my left and in front--an elderly Bajan man said loudly:

Chapter 9: The Flower Forest

"I love the English, you don't queue here, you just push your way on, you push people out of the way--I love England, I love the English"

He seemed to be making fun of me, and rather annoyed, I shouted at him:

"Well you're queuing now!"

(Maybe I should have said: 'how would you like it if I pushed your mother out of the way?'). He retorted back to me:

"Well, normally I push my way on, I push people aside"

I'd like to see someone push him out of the way--or on the floor. The man, to his credit, had not reacted angrily, and I like the Bajan people for not being so easily provoked--though he was old and short with a walking stick; which aren't exactly advantages in any altercation.

In a short while, the bus dropped us at a sign that read 'Flower Forest'. Again it was out in the sticks, hardly anything around except the sea in the distance. Dawn said she didn't really like this, being dropped out of sight of where we were going, so you ended up always having to walk along some country road with high grasses, bushes and trees at the sides. Anyway, as if she had just peered into a crystal ball, Dawn was amazingly right in her assumption of what we were about to encounter. But besides the overgrown foliage at the edges of this country lane, there was the added excitement of a road that went steeply up and then down about three times (not particularly welcome in this humidity).

I usually made light of everything…

The lane was like a jungle road, and at one point we were treated to a great view of a faraway undulating landscape. I usually made light of everything that was a little discomforting to us. I mean most tourists would be going somewhere like this by taxi, or in their own hired transport. It's not everybody who travelled on the Bajan bus system (the majority that did were those with a modest budget to live on--like us).

As we were walking, Dawn said to me, she couldn't understand me saying anything about the pushing as we were boarding the bus. Furthermore, I was taking a chance unnecessarily, especially as the children were with us. If we survived the jungle lane, maybe I'd be more careful in future. I told Dawn it annoys me when people do what they did; I'm the same if I hold the door open for someone and they don't acknowledge the fact. Everybody has their little dislikes.

Finally up ahead was the Flower Forest entrance. It felt like we had already been through a flower forest to get here. I could see one or two vehicles parked outside, so there were a few other people who had thought this place sufficiently interesting to come and see. The entrance fee was £4 each for Dawn and me, half price for the children. I expected a good show for this expenditure. Food and drink was a little more expensive than normal here. Inside, on the left of the entrance and eating area--partly open to the air on the garden side--was a souvenir shop, but all the goods were way over priced for me. Later on I would be proved correct, as I looked around cautiously, and Dawn (in a wild Ivana Trump spending spree mood) bought an ash tray.

Dawn and I took two umbrellas and two walking sticks from the racks, as we began our little trek through this flower forest. I said that the sticks would come in handy for batting any big spiders or insects out of the way. According to the information sheet I had, there were many different kinds of plants here, no doubt of great interest to lovers of plants; but I don't think Dawn was all that impressed, and I agreed with her when she said she had expected a lot more colour.

We walked down a fairly narrow pathway that took us between great leafy plants and breadfruit trees that looked like Triffids, or giant daffodil bulbs just starting to sprout. Moving on further, there were small tree size plants all around us, covered in needle like thorns about two inches long. I touched one of them with my walking stick--and the needles stuck firmly in the wood! I said to Dawn and the children to be careful not to get near those, they would certainly injure you badly if you fell against them.

In a short while, we came to a lookout point with a fairly breathtaking view, and took a few assorted pictures before moving on down the trail. Not much further on, I came upon a gazebo (which is really just a posh name for a shelter that looks very much like the bandstands you see in parks sometimes). I knew this was a gazebo because that's what it said in the information sheet.

The needles stuck firmly in the wood

Chapter 9: The Flower Forest

A lot of the plant names and their positions in the forest were written down for us--but we were not so keen as to search out and identify them all. Some gained our attention more easily than others. Sweeping down from the gazebo was a nice hillside that lent itself well as an impressive backdrop for more pictures of Michelle and Sarah posing happily.

Trekking on through the foliage, we discovered a large plant with red and white flowers on it (they were similar to tulips). A humming bird hovered around the flowers, it flitted quickly from one to the next; and although Dawn tried to get in position to take a picture, she was not successful. The humming bird went away. When it suddenly came back, by the time Dawn had got the camera ready again, the bird had moved on somewhere else.

Just past the point where we saw the humming bird, there was another scenic area. Most of the Flower Forest could be described as hill like, even steep in some places. At this part there were some trees that looked like eighty foot hedges, but it must have been an effect caused by what appeared to be creepers growing en mass all the way up them. Continuing on for a short walk took us to the end of the Flower Forest trail.

We now came in to the main building from the opposite side of the entrance into the Flower Forest. Dawn and I deposited our umbrellas and sticks--which had been of little use to us, except on the steep hills, where they had come in handy to push ourselves up--back where they had come from. I remarked to

Dawn we were like old people using those sticks to help us around (how on earth would real old people get on here?). It was said you could see the forest in about forty-five minutes; I suppose it took us about fifty or fifty-five because we stopped here and there. People could take all day if they wanted to, and just sit around; an option the elderly might prefer. I thought we made it through fairly quickly--maybe we didn't appreciate the plants enough.

As soon as the four of us sat down at a table, Dawn wanted to go straight into the gift shop, and Michelle asked me for chicken and chips. I was trying to conserve money, I mean we would be having a lovely--though simple--dinner, cooked most probably by Dawn (who else was there, it wasn't like there was a servant provided) later on. I said to Michelle to just get some chips then. Where Sarah had sat down at the table, a great long, wide plant leaf was hanging like a canopy above her head; she held it down so it looked like a big hat. I could hear Michelle at the counter asking for chicken and chips; she must have thought I would pay for it anyway. This got me a little angry, and although I tried to talk reasonably to my daughter, she got stroppy and would not accept what I said. I pulled her round a corner out of sight from another group of people sitting nearby--and told her off.

As Michelle walked back to order chips only, I began to think that maybe I was being unfair, so called after her to order the chicken as well (yes, I do have a conscience after all). I can go without food quite often, but I shouldn't expect the children to do the same, especially as when Michelle asks for something, she usually eats all of it--unlike Sarah. It seemed a long while before Michelle's food was ready, and the sound of eating brought new activity to our table. Sarah noticed something moving on the ground near us, and she exclaimed to Michelle that it was a 'centimeter'. We laughed because it was really a centipede.

I was thinking that if there was time, we could visit 'Harrison's Cave' nearby. But Dawn did not want to entertain the idea of moving a bit sharply to see other incredible sights. Dawn was going to take it easy now, and spend ages sitting around relaxing with a cigarette or two. She felt that this would be quite enough excitement for one day, and we shouldn't try to fit in too much. I like to see places and make the most of my holiday; for Dawn, sitting around doing nothing for a long time was making the most of it. Of course, the day wasn't quite over yet, as there were still a few more exertions and bus rides to fit in, before settling down to a peaceful evening at our apartment.

When everybody was ready, we began our trek down the lane back to the bus stop. The road undulated steeply up and then down all the way, as we progressed in a half-shuffling, half-walking movement. Dawn commented that it reminded her of when she climbed Mount Fuji, in Japan; except that the mountain was a continuously steep hill (this was not unusual for a mountain). Climbing Mount Fuji had made Dawn's eyes water, or cry as she put it. The heat sapped our energy fairly quickly. Sarah wanted carrying at these inappropriate moments, and so I would become almost as sapped as Dawn. Michelle tended to drag her feet a bit on our short route marches, but it was noticeable that anytime we were on the beach or swimming in the sea, her energy and enthusiasm knew no limits. If given the choice, Michelle would probably stay in the water for five or six hours without coming out, like a mermaid; and in her new costume Dawn had bought her just the other day, she looked the belle of the beach.

I remarked to Dawn as we walked, I had seen pretty much the same sort of foliage--mostly big green plants--down the lane, as I had paid to see in the Flower Forest. They call it the Flower Forest, but it was certainly not a forest of flowers; there were so many different kinds of trees, including Breadfruit trees, and they're not flowers--even I know that. Also, the view down the lane through one of the hedges, of a large valley like landscape, was almost equal to the scenic lookout point trumpeted by the Flower Forest guide book. Although the visit had been enjoyable, I was sometimes of the opinion 'you pays your money and takes your chances'.

Twenty minutes later we reached the main road where the bus had dropped us. There wasn't a bus stop anywhere around, but as Dawn said, if they could drop you off here--they could also pick you up. Cars drove past every few minutes, beeping when they came near because where we were standing was actually on a corner, and the Bajans always beep their horns if their vision's not good, to warn other drivers.

A tired looking cow came wandering down the lane, across the road in front of us, from the same direction we had just come from. It stopped in the middle of the main road right on the corner, and Dawn became worried in case the animal got hit by a car. Then I saw a Bajan woman walking down the lane behind the cow, and Dawn said (loud enough I thought the woman would hear):

"Oh, look, it's alright, it's with someone"

Well, when the cow stopped, the woman carried on walking past it and down the road. Dawn became concerned again, even so much as walking out into the road to get the cow to move out of harm's way. I said to Michelle Dawn will end up getting run over and the cow will be alright (silly cow).

Anyway, a bus soon arrived and it did stop for us (unlike the other day). Usually the time we caught our buses to go home was about the same time the Bajan schoolchildren were coming out, and there were always a lot of them on board with us. Our first bus would take us to Bridgetown, the second to the Esso station nearby Sandrift Apartments. It was only a quarter of a mile on from where the bus had picked us up, when I saw the sign for 'Harrison's Cave', virtually a short walk away if there had been time. When we arrived back at the Esso station, Dawn and I decided to visit the mini-mart to pick up some food supplies. Our purchase included frozen chicken fillets, mixed veg, bread, cakes, donuts, and fruit juice.

Dawn and I always feel tired when we get back to the apartment, just wanting to sit down for a while and relax. Michelle and Sarah appear to be at their busiest during this time. Michelle bothers Dawn continuously, and Sarah and Michelle always find something to fight about. There is no television, no radio (though Dawn has a radio), and we don't go anywhere in the evenings, so they have to make their own entertainment--If you can call fighting with each other entertainment. This usually involves a game of charades and animal, mineral, or vegetable (Sarah, Michelle, and Dawn).

Dawn is cooking the dinner every night now. Occasionally she says something to me like:

"You're having a rest then?"

Dawn says it's really hot standing at the cooker. I know, I tried it once when we first arrived here, and now I prefer laying down relaxing in front of the air-conditioning in our bedroom. I have to think of my health--if I get ill, who's going to organize us and get things done? I do the washing up anyway, using one of the socks they gave me on the plane.

I spend a considerable amount of my time in the evenings telling Michelle and Sarah to behave themselves. I suppose it's all the excitement of being on holiday, though Michelle is sometimes silly on purpose when she's talking to Dawn. Dawn's sitting there trying to relax, engaged in one of her favourite pastimes of chain smoking for intermediates, while Michelle keeps badgering her, asking meaningless questions--which may be fun for Michelle, but its Chinese water torture for Dawn. Dawn takes the insistent pressure with the tolerance of a mature mind,

Chapter 9: The Flower Forest

only snapping now and again to tell Michelle what an aggravating nuisance she is.

We're having a quiet day tomorrow at the beach. I suggested to Dawn that it might be a good idea to catch a bus and go further up the coast to the St. James area, where legend has it the beaches are better still. Without too much trouble I found myself floating away into the upper stratosphere--where most of my ideas came from--and would not rise out of bed until early the next day. As for Michelle, Sarah, and Dawn, well who knows how their games had ended; all I could hear as I drifted off was Michelle's voice tormenting Dawn.

Chapter
10

THE BEACH AT HOLETOWN

On this fine and sunny morning I wanted to get up very early, as I had done the previous day, then sit once again undisturbed out on the balcony, writing up my diary while watching the birds feed on our rice left overs, or slices of white bread. But due to sleeping a little late last night, I don't feel like rising too early. The thought occurs to me that soon half the day will be gone--as a wise man once said.

By the time I do get up, it's nearly 0800hr. Sarah has awoken also, as if she misses me when I go. Dawn and Michelle always rise an hour or more later than the little one and myself. Then Dawn likes to lie down again after she's had breakfast--what a life! Dawn always has cornflakes and milk, so does Sarah; but Sarah can keep asking three or four times, leaving

Chapter 10: The Beach at Holetown

Dawn wondering what's happening to her cereal. One time Dawn had a big old fruit bowl full of cornflakes and milk. When I saw her eating that, I remarked no wonder the cornflakes were going so fast, if she's eating great big bowls full. Dawn said there wasn't very much in it, it wasn't full (though still about three normal bowls worth).

After breakfast I go into the bathroom. When I'm finished and need toilet paper, there is not enough left. I tell Dawn and Michelle to go and ask the manageress for some more, but they say she isn't downstairs and won't answer the phone. Sarah's laughing and turning the bathroom light on and off from outside. I said I'm going to get her when I come out. She laughs and carry's on doing it

"I'm going to spend the day in the toilet" I say.

"We're not; we're going to the beach" Dawn replies.

We laugh. In the end I just use a Barbados visitor's newspaper, which is provided to help the tourists while they are here.

While I was in the bathroom, Dawn and I had an argument about who's been using the paper. Dawn said I should have checked to see how much was left (this reminded me of the Dave Allen sketch, where he says nobody ever looks to see how much is left before they go). The fact is that a new roll had been installed yesterday and I never went to use any of it until now, then only a few sheets because that's all that was there.

It was funny because Sarah wanted to go a little later, and she had to use the Barbados Visitor also--when I turned the light out she didn't like it.

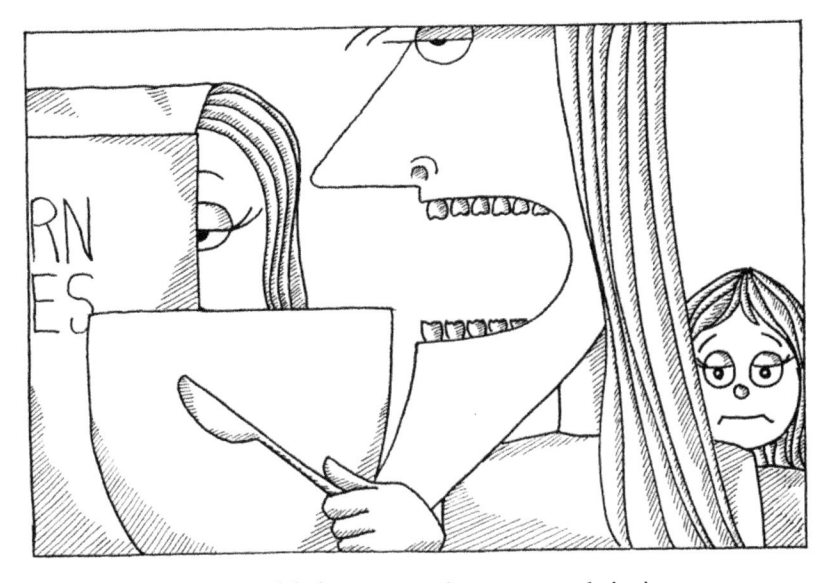

Dawn said there wasn't very much in it

Our friendly manageress had told me that the bus going to Speight town would take us to St. James. Speight town itself was a long way further up the coast. Dawn and I liked travelling on the big blue buses and smaller yellow ones because they never messed us around. I said to Dawn we would look out for a nice spot on the way.

Presently, our bus entered a place called Hole Town (I wonder where it got its name from; I couldn't even see one hole). This appeared to be a good area; clean, modern buildings, shopping mall, and just where we got off the bus was a large green and white building--that turned out to be the police station.

Chapter 10: The Beach at Holetown

Dawn said this made her feel safe. The police building contained a museum and some other facility also. We walked past the side of the station, which quickly led us down to the beach. It looked okay, plenty of activity. Judging by the number of nice hotels with gardens opening out onto the sand, this must have been one of the more popular localities.

The four of us made our way up the beach, searching for a suitable spot to settle down for a few hours. Dawn, Michelle, and Sarah always took their shoes and socks off as soon as they hit the sand. I resolutely kept mine on until we found a place to stop. Although I could see how far the waves were reaching up the beach, and kept what I estimated to be a safe distance between them and my feet, every once in a while the sea would decide to make one big effort and stretch a bit further; which resulted in me getting a booty or two. This was to happen a few times.

I said to Dawn I had to have a spot with some shade from the sun if I needed it. Dawn didn't seem to mind much about shade; she was coated in factor fifteen sunscreen, most vividly on her face; and I would sometimes sing Phantom of the Opera to her. Dawn put plenty of the cream on her body as well, so had no fear of being burnt. I didn't have sun cream, but Dawn was so kind as to let me use hers. Up till now, I had been putting a little on my nose and forehead only because if my nose gets too burnt, it can blister and there is a risk of infection. But today I smoothed some on: shoulders, arms, chest, neck, and legs, fearing prolonged exposure on a hot day like this could cause me some problems; possibly as bad as those in the Philippines a few years ago, when languidly floating just under the surface of the water proved to be not as safe as I thought, resulting in a worse sunburn than if I had been out. According to Dawn, this stuff was water resistant (so was the Titanic).

Anyway, later on that evening back at the apartment, I found myself turning a brighter shade of red in all the usual areas. Dawn and I have to be careful not to become Barbados Kentucky Fried Chickens in this tropical sun, but Michelle and Sarah can bounce around the beach all day, splash and swim in the sea for as long as they want to; and at the end of it, still come out with only a bit more of a lovely golden tan. It's all I can do to play peek-a-boo from behind the nearest tree.

There were other people with white bodies; I wondered whether they would get burnt. Dawn said this is what she liked, a nice beach with people around; she felt safer and more relaxed here. It was okay, but in the shade under some trees, next to a little pond like area, there were hundreds of ants weaving about. They must be keeping out of the sun themselves, but it meant if I sat there in the shade, I would start getting them all over me. I didn't know which was worse--frying in the sun or having ants pouring over you.

Chapter 10: The Beach at Holetown

I didn't know which was worse...

After an hour or so, a small chocolate Bajan lady came churning the sand up on the beach, asking if we wanted the girls' hair braided. Without telling me the price, she had asked if I wanted the whole head done. Then I asked how much, and the Bajan beach to beach (as in door to door) saleswoman told me £12 for the whole head or B2 per braid (approx. 70p). So Michelle had two done and the woman did a third saying she could have it free--only mentioning this after noticing I was about to protest; how about the other one (Sarah), did she want two as well?

"No, just one" I said.

I reckoned this lady was pulling a fast one, doing one braid for free for Michelle so she could recoup the money on doing two for Sarah. I was pleased with myself, paying for three braids and getting four, maybe my gullibility was behind me now; if so, knowing my luck, it was sure to catch up soon.

The small beach bead saleswoman finished the braiding very quickly, time was of the essence; this was such a lucrative business, and there were so many more dope's hair to braid before the sun went down, and she skipped all the way to the bank to deposit her sacks of money. The final touches involved putting a bit of silver foil on the end of the braid, with two coloured beads of your choice. A minute later, Sarah or Michelle accidently knocked her big plastic bag of beads over, and they all poured out onto the sand. I helped put them back. Maybe in the end there was more sand than beads. It had cost me £2 for four braids.

I saw two young white girls, about six and eight years old with all their hair braided, so I'm sure the bead lady can often make buckets of money in a day--if she doesn't lose all her beads in the sand. Dawn told me that the braidy lady had been asking her first (this must have been while I was in the sea with Sarah and Michelle, and Dawn was on the beach soaking up the sun); she kept telling her 'no', and eventually, our friend understood the message these two letters of the alphabet conveyed, when aligned in this order.

At the end of the afternoon, the sky started clouding over and the sun began to partially hide itself, in a prelude to the real disappearing act soon to

Chapter 10: The Beach at Holetown

be performed. We covered up our swimming costumes because although the bajans were not prudish, they expected people to walk around in bathing costumes only on the beach. We crossed the road to visit the shopping mall, but crazy as it may seem to you or I, the shops had closed at four o'clock. Only the supermarket was open, so Dawn and I went in for supplies.

Michelle and Sarah saw the cake and donut counter, and then Sarah badgered me continuously to buy some as I pottered about trying to get together a good combination for dinner. We bought potatoes, broccoli, fruit juice; non-fat cheese slices amongst other things, and of course--cake. Dawn bought a few plums (that's how she got her telephone voice).

A bus came almost straight away, and as usual it was full at this time of day; but that doesn't stop more people getting on, they just have to travel like us--standing room only. Sarah almost disappears from view, she's so small. The bus driver stops and starts suddenly; it's hard to remain upright, but we manage and before long we're back at our favourite bus stop again.

In the apartment Dawn says don't lock the bottom of the balcony doors because she can't unlock them very easily. I tell her I should because if somebody tries to get in it's harder for them with the two locks. Dawn said:

"Oh Mark, don't say that"

"Well you have to think of these things" I replied.

Michelle's voice suddenly crackled onto the airwaves with the observation:

"Thinking of things like putting your trousers under the mattress to iron them Daddy?"

The story behind this remark originated from a brainwave I had earlier in the day, when I put my newly hand washed trousers under my mattress to flatten them because Dawn's travel iron had a travel plug that didn't work. The story behind this unsatisfactory state of affairs being that, on her last holiday it got changed over by mistake with one of her friend's travel plugs (I suppose her friend is wondering how come her plug works). I had asked Michelle to remind me not to forget my trousers were there when we were going home. They didn't look any better when I took them out anyway, so that idea was a waste of time. Dawn said all I had to do was hang them up properly while they were drying.

Dawn cooked a nice dinner for us of mashed potato, broccoli, chicken fillet and rice. This was the best meal I've enjoyed so far. It's been pouring of rain for at least an hour, and the time is now 1955hr. Dawn said the rain will bring out all the 'mozzies' when it stops. I said hopefully when they come out they would all have been drowned.

Chapter 11

MILLIONS OF RAINDROPS

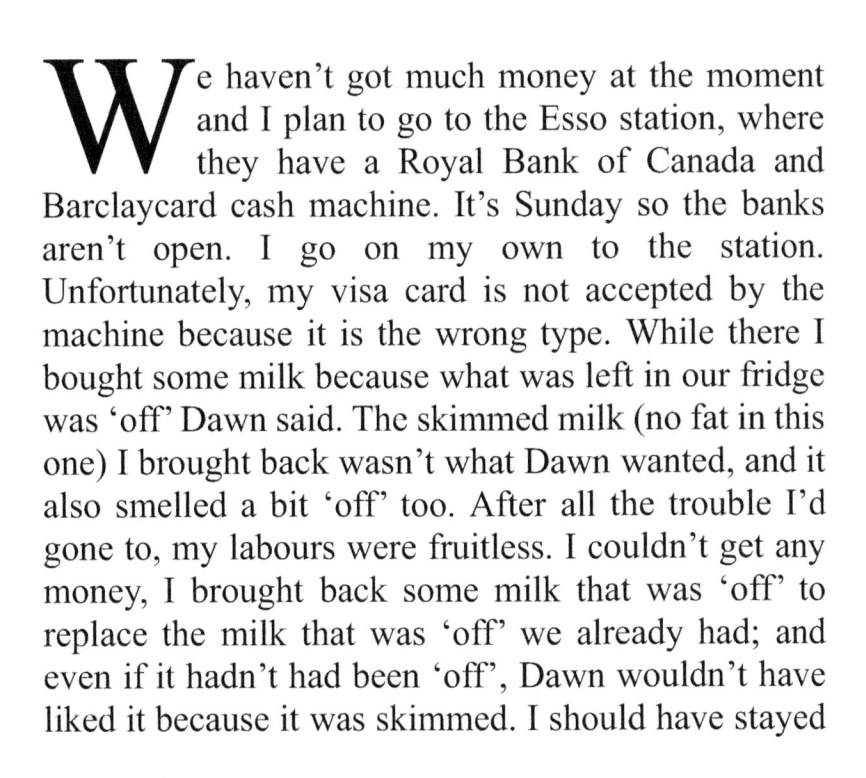

We haven't got much money at the moment and I plan to go to the Esso station, where they have a Royal Bank of Canada and Barclaycard cash machine. It's Sunday so the banks aren't open. I go on my own to the station. Unfortunately, my visa card is not accepted by the machine because it is the wrong type. While there I bought some milk because what was left in our fridge was 'off' Dawn said. The skimmed milk (no fat in this one) I brought back wasn't what Dawn wanted, and it also smelled a bit 'off' too. After all the trouble I'd gone to, my labours were fruitless. I couldn't get any money, I brought back some milk that was 'off' to replace the milk that was 'off' we already had; and even if it hadn't had been 'off', Dawn wouldn't have liked it because it was skimmed. I should have stayed

Chapter 11: Millions of Raindrops

in bed.

If I'd been able to get some money we could have gone to the Wildlife Reserve, but now Dawn and I decide we'll stay here instead. At 1400hr the four of us make our way down to the beach. There were a few people around, probably because it was a Sunday. We started picking up seashells; there were not as many as you might expect lying around, and most of those were very small.

Before long it began to rain. Dawn wants to go back--she doesn't want to catch pneumonia she states emphatically. I don't suppose she would have. I walk into the sea gleefully for a swim, keeping my tent sized blue t-shirt on. Then I realize my pen is in my back pocket. I know I put my number two notebook there also, but it's not there now. I look for it in the sea (I must have a good chance of finding it). Not being very successful, I get out of the water to search the bag with the shells and footwear in. What do you know, it's not there either. I go back into the water (presumably there was a part of the sea I hadn't looked in) and suddenly, appearing from under my shirt is the little lost notebook, all soggy with ink literally running off the pages. I take the book out and place it in our bag on the beach, hoping there is a possibility I can salvage the words later.

Michelle and I stay in the sea for another half an hour after Dawn takes Sarah back to the apartment. The rain is really coming down, and Michelle and I are only warm while in the water. I notice millions of little raindrops as they break on the surface, looking quite pretty falling into the sea for miles around me. After a while we walk back up the hill like two drowned rats. Michelle commented we didn't need to wash the sand off our feet, as the rain had already done so.

Dawn and Sarah are now dry and having a rest. Michelle goes for a shower, while I, sopping, dripping wet, sit down at our glass dinner table and begin an attempt to salvage book two of my diary. Hunched over the little sodden pages, I peer diligently into the swirling blue mists of ink and water that form a mosaic like pattern. Somehow managing to see something, I write it out word by word and progress to about six pages worth. As it becomes more difficult to see the words under the lounge light, I move over by the fridge, and seeing more clearly under the ceiling light overhead--which is brighter in this smaller area--I continue with my work.

I'm soaked, it's still raining, I'm struggling with this pen and my eyes, and what happens--all the lights go out! Hey presto, we have a blackout. No electricity--nothing. In the Philippines, 'brownouts' as they are called, are quite common in medium priced hotels, but I didn't expect to encounter them here. Luckily we have a candle, and Dawn soon lights it because she needs to go to the bathroom. I transfer my papers and notebook from the top of the fridge to a chair placed just inside the balcony doors (which I opened to let more light in, but not for long as it's starting to get dark). Still pouring rain outside and a slight breeze blows the pages if I'm not careful. As the only light (bar our candle) begins to fade, I write out

Chapter 11: Millions of Raindrops

some more of my diary.

We don't have much in the way of supplies at the moment and Dawn suggests I could go and get some. I say I might walk to the petrol mini-mart. Dawn recommends the other one (Uncle Tom's cabin type mini-mart, Indian corner shop, but run by Bajan people--one who is half as wide as the store itself). I asked why. Dawn replied because it was closer. I said:

"Well, it just means I'll get soaking wet over a shorter distance".

When the light is so bad I can't write any more, I go down to see the manageress to speak to her about our predicament. In the pouring rain (which doesn't matter because I'm soaking wet already) I walk barefoot down to the office. Our host opens the door in the enfolding darkness--except for a solitary candle on the counter--and reassures me the blackout should only last fifteen or twenty minutes. Suddenly the lights come back on again and I can see her.

I told the manageress we had broken a glass (Dawn) and I would pay for it. Our host said it didn't matter--and did I want some more? (What to break?). I took two and also asked if there were any washing up pads, as I couldn't find them in the shops. The manageress replied they didn't actually supply those, but she brought me a spare one from out of what looked like a broom cupboard at the back of her office. I thought I could hear a television in there. Most probably she lived in a little box room, with a couple of cans of baked beans and a big pile of receipts dating back to 1960--the last one before ours being 1982 (well she did say this area wasn't very popular).

As soon as I return to our room it stops raining. I walk in singing 'happy days are here again'. First I have to have a shower (as if the water that's engulfed me already today wasn't enough). Dawn cooked a good meal of potatoes, mixed vegetables, chicken fillets and rice. I enjoyed a few donuts after, and a couple of beers; we always have plenty of soft drinks too. Michelle and Sarah still fight with each other a lot. They both antagonize Dawn (also me of course) and she was a bit put out by what happened to her boiled sweet she had left unwrapped on her bed, ready to eat when she came out the bathroom. On returning to her bed Dawn suspected something, and asked us if someone had touched her sweet. It turned out Sarah had picked the sweet up and sucked it for a while--then put it back again.

Chapter

12

THE WILDLIFE RESERVE

Today our plan is to go to Bridgetown, visit the bank, withdraw some money on my Barclaycard, and then catch a bus to the Wildlife Reserve. I get up fairly early, about 0730hr, on this our ninth day in Barbados. It's best if we get organized a little sooner than normal, so that there will be enough time to visit the bank first and then the Wildlife Reserve. The Reserve is near the north coast of Barbados--a fair distance from Sandrift. Starting from Bridgetown, I expect this will be a comparatively long journey, with the bus actually passing our bus stop at Black Rock, and then travelling along the coastal road to Speight town; from where it will veer to the right and thereafter take us inland towards the Reserve.

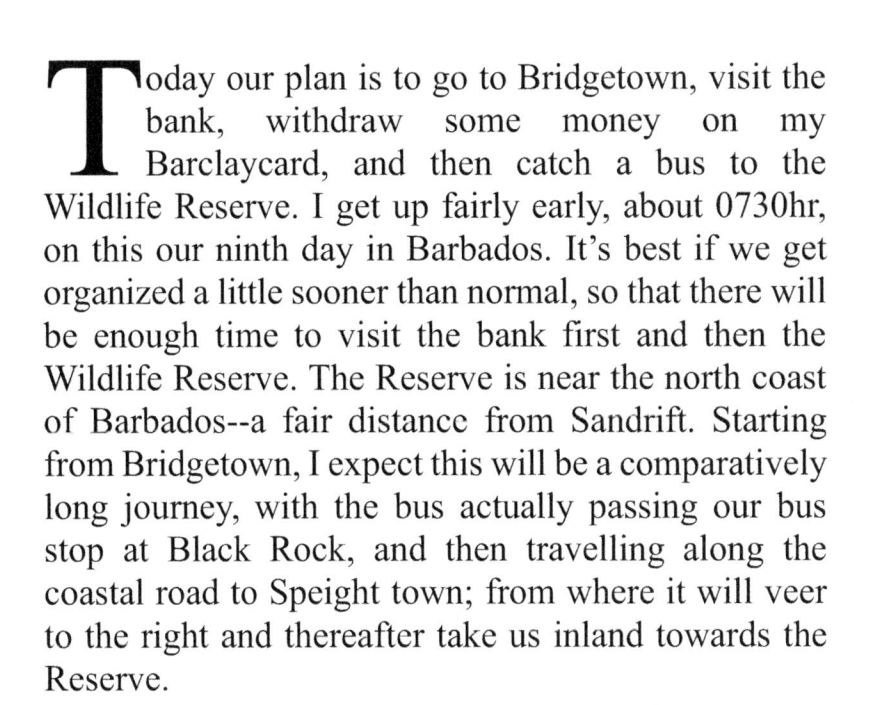

Chapter 12: The Wildlife Reserve

We left our apartment in good time (1100hr). As the four of us strode towards the bus stop, the weather was fine and we were looking forward to an enjoyable day out. Shortly, a bus arrived and took us to Bridgetown--at the Jubilee Bus Station end. I stepped down onto the pavement and asked Dawn and Michelle to cross to the other side of the street, so I could walk in the shade. I popped in and out of one or two shops, mainly to see if I could find Michelle any of those baggy trousers in her size--but there were none.

Just around the corner was a Barclays Bank, perfect for the visa card. In side we were confronted with a dauntingly long queue. If I had to join it we could have been all morning, but in one far corner there was a foreign exchange counter which dealt with transactions such as the one I wanted to make. After the process, the staff told me I should collect my money from one of the cashiers, which lie not at the end of a rainbow--but at the end of an excruciatingly long and winding, slowly moving queue. You'd think they were giving something away for free (which is impossible for a bank of course). I mentioned the queue to the staff at the foreign exchange counter (while picking my lower jaw up from the carpet) and they--realizing my distress--then said they would do it for me. As a result of this act of kindness, we were not in the bank very long.

Curiously, I wasn't given a receipt detailing the exchange rate or cost of the transaction; neither were the staff themselves able to tell me what the cost to me was likely to be. What the bank did have was a direct link to visa to simply obtain money. The rate was 3.2 Bajan dollars to the pound--slightly more than I had calculated to Dawn.

The Jubilee Bus Station was only around the corner from the bank. Dawn said that there were two destinations to look out for, but we couldn't see either of the buses at the moment. I had some of Dawn's factor 15 on my nose, but it was still too hot to stand in the open all the time. I kept trying to keep in the shade. It was good not having to worry about Michelle and Sarah in that respect. I bought a few drinks at the garden shed sized refreshment bar. When you're moving about outside in this heat, you always feel thirsty.

We were waiting at the place where the big blue buses stopped, but as I said to Dawn, there were smaller yellow one's going around us and down the road. It looked as if they stopped a little further on by some traffic lights. I noticed that one of these buses displayed a destination Dawn had mentioned earlier. I decided it would be best for us to stand somewhere in the middle where we could see the blue buses parking up, but also still be close enough to run and catch a yellow one when it stopped.

I stood in the shadow of a tall palm tree and kept my eyes open--even so, it was Dawn who first saw our yellow bus, and we all hot footed it to what I correctly deduced to be a bus stop. I asked the driver if he was going to the Wildlife Reserve:

Chapter 12: The Wildlife Reserve

"Yeah boy, get in" he said.

We climbed aboard, and for the first time sat at the back. A mile down the road it started to rain. Not more than a few minutes ago, I had been sheltering warily from the gaze of a hot sun; now it was all I could do to close the window and avoid getting wet. Anyway I thought, if it rains on the way to the reserve, maybe it will have stopped by the time we arrive.

Barbados Diary

COCONUT

I forgot to mention the coconut I couldn't break

Though I gave it my best throw, stamp, and shake

All my efforts were in vain

As I flexed my muscles to take the strain

This damn coconut was a hard nut to crack

If anything would break, it'd be my back

I dropped it from three floors up, to smash on the ground

But running to examine it--a whole coconut's all I found

I hit it with the solid lump of coral we picked up off the beach

Hoping to shatter this hard food, so we'd have a piece each

But it was still resistant to every ploy I used

What to do next I thought, it's leaving me confused

Then Michelle took it outside, and in a moment returned

With a great big smile on her face, the coconut was nicely split

…I learned

Chapter 12: The Wildlife Reserve

The bus travelled up past our Esso station, Hole Town, and further still to Speight Town--unseen territory for us--then across some hilly country side, finally stopping in front of a battered sign proclaiming 'Wildlife Reserve'. The conductor pointed to a side road leading off into the distance, and said it was a little way down there. Stepping down from the bus, we began the route march. It did look a bit far, and I couldn't see anything on the horizon that might indicate a 'Wildlife Reserve'. After a couple of minutes, a small mini-van pulled up alongside and the driver asked us if we would like a lift, as it was still a while yet to the Reserve. The man was Bajan, on his own, and had the appearance of someone who didn't need to hustle us for anything; just offering a natural friendliness.

Accepting the lift, it wasn't long before I realized how much further it was than I had guessed. I said to Dawn that the bus is supposed to be dropping you at the Wildlife Reserve, yet you're still a long way from it. When the mini-van driver dropped us off, he said we should just follow the track that led up to a small forest like area on a hill. Opposite the track--on the other side of the road--was a recreation ground I was told. I had visions of going there later (but as it happened, there would not be enough time).

Dawn and I thanked the man for the lift and started up the rough, rocky track. Some workers in a field on our right stopped to have a look at us; maybe they thought we were film stars, who knows. Then, in front was an entrance with a sign Dawn read first. This was The Wildlife Reserve. It was sort of inconspicuous, not noticeable until you came right up to it. There was nothing inconspicuous about the price though. To get to this truly wonderful Noah's Ark of God's finest, most cherished, and exciting, all singing, all dancing creatures (for I reasoned, that's what it certainly must be for the money they were asking), it would cost the princely sum of £7 for adults, and half price for the children. Children probably meant up to the age of six months knowing this lot. The final toll reached a monumental £18.

"It must be good for that amount" I said (my bottom lip trembling, as I looked down inconsolably).

We were given a little diagram explaining what could be found in the Reserve, and how anybody--village idiots included (why, I've never been so insulted by a Bajan Wildlife Reserve leaflet)--could get around. On the ground in front of us were some rather big tortoises, walking freely on the paths (maybe they wanted to take a look around the Reserve as well). Apparently that was the idea of this place--for visitors to walk amongst the animals in their natural habitat. Sarah went straight to a tortoise, stroking the head and talking to it, as she had with the smaller ones at the zoo. Dawn wanted to take some pictures of Michelle and Sarah with the tortoise, but it moved too quickly for her to get in position for a shot. Eventually, Dawn managed some success when breaking her personal land speed record.

Looking at the pathway through the reserve on the diagram, it did not seem possible to simply follow one path and see everything. Visitors would need to

Chapter 12: The Wildlife Reserve

sometimes go off in other directions, and then come back again to rejoin the original path before continuing. We left the tortoise to do whatever tortoises do in the afternoons and set foot on the pathway. Michelle and Sarah would see other tortoises along the route, as apparently there were more of these big, red legged ones here in the reserve, than in the rest of Barbados. For the first fifty yards or so, expecting to see a spider, an alligator--anything really--I didn't see a dickey boo. Then, all at once, we came upon more tortoises and crocodiles, or alligators--I didn't get close enough to tell the difference--in a pond. To the right of the pond was a path leading through a huge cage, with squawking birds evidently the main occupants.

I left the bird house for the moment, electing to continue up the path we were on, which appeared to be taking us around the edge of the reserve. Many plants and bushes boarded either side of the track. A little further along, on our left, set up against the perimeter fence, was a building made from large stones. I thought the windows looked rather odd. It was a bit like a cave inside, very spacious, but without too much in it. The building was half museum and half information center, with a few items laid out in a couple of display cabinets, and some ecology documents posted on the walls. The documents were mostly about the research being carried out on monkeys, explaining in the process how necessary it all was. Of most interest to Dawn, was the occupant of a large 'Tweety Pie' bird cage that lay on the floor at the right hand side, as we went through the entrance.

The cage was of a heavy construction, designed in a spiral, creeper like fashion, as most of the other metal work in the building was also. The large anaconda head within looked somewhat too big to be living there. It was a silent giant that slithered slowly into a new position. Dawn was very eager about having her picture taken close to this creature, exhorting me to quickly get a snap before it moved away, and the big, ugly, smirking head couldn't be seen so clearly--and the snake's head could not be seen either. There was so much of the cage that the snake did not show itself as well as we would have liked, but I got a couple of shots I'm sure Dawn will treasure forever. You'd think she was having her picture taken with Richard Gere.

Back of an otter's head

Outside, at the end of this building, we came upon a little rockery with a pool of water in the middle of it. A girl member of staff was feeding some otters that were waiting hungrily by the rockery. When they

Chapter 12: The Wildlife Reserve

got the fish from the girl, the otters took it inside a pipe that went into the ground alongside the rockery, then came out again--with the fish--and started eating it in the pool. They hold the food in their little, human like hands, and eat as if constantly licking bits of meat from between their teeth. These animals look somewhat like cats, with their whiskers and feline features. The otters kept scurrying into the pipe and coming out with another fish, looking at us, and holding the fish delicately in their hands whilst chomping away. They didn't seem to mind our efforts to get close by them in order to obtain a memorable picture, but it was made so difficult because the otters couldn't keep still long enough to be in the family album. But I believe there will be some photos with the back of an otter's head and a smiling Michelle (I don't know which looks better).

Grandson of Kong

There were some monkeys making an

appearance on this part of the track as well. Carrying Sarah, I tried to maneuver close enough for Dawn to get a snap of a monkey and Sarah. The monkey seemed offended, snarled a bit and swiped his paw out. Okay, they're only little monkeys (very like Sarah), but we both recoiled quickly, or en tout de suite as the French might say. Dawn had kept saying she could only get the monkey in, can't get both of them. Sure, and then, while waiting for the photographer to take what you would think was a relatively simple picture, a paw from the spiteful ape swipes out maliciously again at our heads--grandson of Kong gets mad--can you get that in Dawn?

Coming to the end of the path, we went back in at the start once more, to see the areas we hadn't seen the first time around. There were some pelicans standing by the side of the track, and although I was going to take a picture of Dawn standing next to them, it didn't work out; this was because either I couldn't get everybody in, or Dawn hadn't told me whereabouts she was standing amongst the pelicans.

A little further along was the big aviary like cage we'd come upon earlier. When I cautiously opened the door and led the way inside, unsurprisingly, it was occupied by many different kinds of birds. Monkeys bounced around on the outside of the cage. The notice said you may see a rat in there (surely news to attract the crowds in droves). How wonderful, a member of the rodent family, presumably eating with a knife and fork at the dinner table. We did see a rat, and actually it wasn't a highlight of our visit. The rat was lying on its

Chapter 12: The Wildlife Reserve

back and dying for some reason--to be honest I didn't care much anyway. Maybe he couldn't take it any longer, being in here with all these birds--it gets to you after a while.

Slowly but surely, it began to rain. Other people had umbrellas, but not us. Dawn and I hadn't seen any when we came in, and didn't realize they were available. At The Flower Forest, we were provided with umbrellas and walking sticks. It didn't rain then and un-be known to them, my leg was much better now, thank you. The only explanation of course was sod's law. To avoid getting too wet, we all went into the cave like building with the anaconda for company. Behind us came other families: French, English, and German. It seemed a different nationality each time.

I stood at the entrance (half in the way I suspect), looking out at what was more like a tropical rainforest now. We were right at the end of the wet season, and this was a reminder that it was not yet over. Hey thanks, with all the dry weather we'd had so far, I thought there might be a chance of escaping another pounding from the rain. In the brochure they don't depict Barbados as Atlantis under water, so you could be unpleasantly surprised to find yourself having to walk around holding an umbrella--which we didn't even have.

A little brown deer crossed the path a few yards from our doorway. It stood still under a bush for a long while, not moving and looking in my direction, as if watching to see whether I might threaten it. The otters emerged from a pipe set into the ground next to the path, and looked to be enjoying themselves scampering about in the rain. The weather didn't improve for a long time, and Dawn was not enjoying herself; getting impatient, suggesting we ought to at least go back to the entrance area where the restaurant was. Eventually, when the rain eased off, Dawn, myself, Michelle, and Sarah walked quickly up the path to the entrance.

On the way, one of the staff passed by us with umbrellas; he was looking for somebody who wanted one, but it wasn't meant to be us. Before the end of the path, near the restaurant, Dawn attempted to get a close up picture of the small brown deer, which had, she said, appeared suddenly on the path in front of her. The rain was still appearing also as we reached the shelter of the little outdoor restaurant. Food and drink prices were of course daylight robbery, and when the light started to fade, it became night time robbery--I needed no encouragement to abstain. Although everything seems so expensive, it is mainly due to the low exchange rate of the pound against the Bajan dollar.

Michelle said she was hungry--which always seems to be the case--and she wanted a jacket potato with all the trimmings. I tried to get her to accept the word 'no', that she could eat when we got back to the apartment (why, we could all eat then). I told Michelle this potato would cost the same as her new baseball style t-shirt (about £4). Our world is full of comparisons I find. Again I eventually relented and let Michelle order what she wanted. Though, as fate would have it, in an ironic conclusion to the jacket-potato

Chapter 12: The Wildlife Reserve

story, the woman behind the counter, who had been listening to us all this time--said she didn't have any. Marvelous.

It was time to go. We came out of the Wildlife Reserve, and then, further up the hill, on the other side of a makeshift car park, I saw part two of our entertainment--the watchtower and some small forest. I didn't know what the watchtower was about yet, aside from the obvious implication of the title; the forest was evidently designed to show the ecology of Barbados. I said to Dawn we might as well get our money's worth out of the tickets (which didn't come as a surprise to Dawn), but I was a bit dubious about how much this next attraction might be worth. In the now incessantly pouring rain--not a lot I suspected.

At the ticket desk, I couldn't produce our tickets that covered for both the Reserve and this area, but the girl let us in anyway; probably because I looked so honest. The girl gave us two great big black umbrellas, and while Dawn went to the toilet in a wooden cabin a few yards away, on the edge of the ecology forest, Michelle, Sarah, and myself went the other way up a short pathway to the watchtower, carrying both the umbrellas.

The watchtower was nothing much inside. I walked up the stairs, pushed a button and listened to the taped voice telling us the history of this tower and the other four or five scattered over the island. The idea was that in the event of invasion they signaled each other, spread the news. There were some photos on the walls, a map, and items in a couple of display cases. We only stayed there a few minutes. All that was left to do was take a walk around the forest of Bajan ecology, but with the rain coming down fairly hard now and all of us being pretty wet, we were really only looking forward to getting back to the apartment.

The rain coming down fairly hard now...

Suddenly the rain came to a stop, and leaving the shelter of the wooden cabin with the toilets in, we started walking down the track to the road again. At the point where the mini-van dropped us off, there was a bus stop. I suggested to Dawn we could wait there, but she said if we walked back to where the bus had left us (stranded it would seem), then our chances of getting another one straight back to Bridgetown would be better. It was agreed that the recreation center was not going to figure in our plans now.

Striding out positively, Dawn and I began the long old walk to the main road. I was carrying Sarah

Chapter 12: The Wildlife Reserve

and joking that a bus would go past as we walked. Michelle lagged behind all the time, lacking in energy for something she didn't really fancy doing. Then I could not believe what I was seeing. It was at least five or six hundred yards to go to the main road. A bus appeared in the distance, and I said to Dawn that if we had gone a little faster and not kept waiting for Michelle, we could have reached the main road in time to catch it. I watched the bus as it reversed back into the road that stretched out ahead of us. Dawn commented it must be turning round to go in the opposite direction. I didn't think so--it looked as if he might be waiting for us. As the bus continued to reverse further down our road than it needed to in order to turn around, I realized that the driver was actually coming all the way down to pick us up.

Dawn and I were astonished, we couldn't believe our luck. As I climbed aboard I was surprised to find that this was the same bus that had dropped us off over two and a half hours ago. I thanked the driver and conductor, talking to them for a while (maybe now they were wishing they hadn't picked us up). This good deed had raised my pleasant mood to a feeling of happiness. Dawn even said that Bajans were mostly helpful. A little backbone had been restored to her wilting faith in Bajan humanity this fine day (well it was now anyway). I could just imagine a 140 bus in Hayes reversing down a side road for a couple of hundred yards to pick up some passengers. Why, in England, the drivers often wait for pensioners to exhaust themselves trying to reach the bus stop before quickly pulling away.

Again school children get on the bus and the atmosphere is lively. After catching another bus from Bridgetown we reach the Esso station, and I do a little shopping there, which includes a lot of donuts. Dawn and I are pleased to get back to our Sandrift apartment. At the end of the day we are always ready to put our feet up and doze off. Of course Dawn has to make the dinner first, and her efforts are very much appreciated. If Michelle and Sarah are tired at all, they don't show it. Every evening they argue with each other as well as play games. It seems that I'm always falling asleep, while the others are awake playing charades or something.

I'd like to stay up late, but the rigours of the day have prepared me for an early night. Dawn ran out of money yesterday--except for what she has put aside for the airport tax and some English money. We will get by alright; I have plenty of breathing space on my Barclaycard. Tomorrow will be our last full day in Barbados, and we are planning to spend it back at the beach in Hole Town, where we went a few days ago. The Wildlife Reserve was our last visit to the island's many tourist attractions, manufactured recently, solely for the purpose of attracting holiday maker's cash and credit cards. Dawn and I would have liked to have seen Harrison's Cave, but it was not to be. At least we went past it a couple of times. The cave was a natural feature of the island, and probably worth a visit, but you never knew with these attractions until you went.

I thought that tomorrow we could go to Bridgetown and shop for a few presents--especially in

Chapter 12: The Wildlife Reserve

Cave Shepherd--then take a trip to Hole Town and the beach later on. But I remembered that there were a lot of shops in Hole Town, including another Cave Shepherd, so here was an opportunity to kill two birds with one stone, so to speak.

Each day we would never leave the apartment before 1100hr, and considering Barbados got dark by 1800hr, it would have been better to start our adventures for the day a few hours earlier. As was Barbados shrouded in a cloak of darkness by six o'clock in the evening, by six in the morning, the cloak had lifted, and in the emerald forest of trees on our balcony side, white butterflies and singing birds were all around. I said to Dawn that when you are only starting, or a few days into your holiday, you have no thoughts about the time when you have to fly back; but a few days before the day of departure, you think more about what you want to do--to get the most out of the time that is left. Michelle and Sarah always loved going to the sea, so we had to get some more of that in. Anytime we visited a tourist attraction, it really required a whole day to do comfortably. I wanted to spend a little more time shopping for gifts before leaving, and the day of our departure we needed plenty of time to prepare, and get ourselves to the airport early for the 1855hr flight. With all this in mind, our last full day would therefore be split between a visit to the sea and shopping. The day of our departure would have to be devoted almost entirely to reaching the airport in good time--so as not to miss the flight.

In golden slumber we slept, undisturbed

through the silent night, only dreams and drifting memories before daylight

Only dreams and drifting memories before daylight…

Chapter

13

'WE DO LIKE TO BE BESIDE THE SEA'

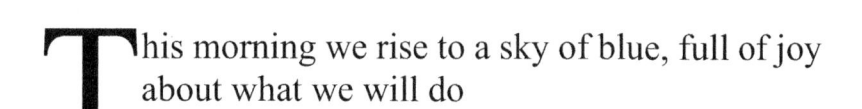

This morning we rise to a sky of blue, full of joy about what we will do

Breakfast goes without a hitch

Then we get ready with our clothes and things, me, Dawn, Michelle

--and 'Titch'

Being a little on the red side, I'll keep my shirt on today at the beach--though shorts are in order to let the air reach my legs. With some sun cream they should do alright, not forgetting dashes on the nose and arms to be safe. Dawn did not want to carry too much in her small shoulder bag, and said she would not bring--amongst other things--both the suntan lotions. It would seem that the extra weight was a

Chapter 13: 'We Do Like to Be Beside the Sea'

problem. With a towel in a plastic carrier bag (this also came in handy for putting the shoes and socks in when the children went swimming), we were just about fully prepared for anything. Dawn always seemed to forget her camera on our trips to the sea--today would be no exception.

Starting with a degree of freshness, as you always do in the first few minutes of a new adventure, Dawn and I led the way up a steep lane to the main road, and then left off the roundabout to the bus stop alongside our favourite Esso station. As usual a bus soon came and we hopped aboard. We travelled along the coastal road for twenty minutes, past little homes on the beach, and every so often a garden shed sized shop with people sitting at the counter. Dawn said that these places must be the equivalent of our local pubs back home. Suddenly I saw the Cave Shepherd store and rang the bell.

Dawn thought that the beach we went to last time must be miles away, but I was certain it was only up the road. As I approached the shopping center, a Bajan man came towards us from our left asking:

"Are you English?"

Why did he think that? Did I have a monocle, brolly, bowler hat, hanky on my head, fish and chips in a newspaper, tattoos, an obvious dislike for Bajan buttheads like him, always asking questions when people are trying to have a holiday--or was my bum hanging out the back of my trousers, 'a la' British builder? I replied:

"Yes, but we have to go, my sister not well..."

And we carried on walking, ignoring him from then on. That niftily disposed of his annoying presence. I knew it best not to engage in conversation, as Dawn had said; if you do, they play you like a fish on a hook and reel you in.

This Cave Shepherd was much smaller than the one in Bridgetown, but like its brother, well air-conditioned and at first glance appeared to have a similar selection of quality goods. After looking around though, I was of the opinion that the t-shirts (amongst other items) were not as good as in Bridgetown. There was also a large section devoted to cheap looking--but not to buy--typical tourist paraphernalia, of the tasteless kind. Bits of shells, ham fistedly glued to sticks and slivers of cloth to approximate a garish figure, somehow, in a hit and miss fashion, designed to represent Barbados--though in what gawky, gooney, clueless, plastic smiled, sausage fingered way, even I failed to see.

Looking at the shelves in this part of the store was not much of a cultural education, but it did serve to heighten my amazement at the extent some people go to in producing hand crafted junk; this being of such low quality, it would embarrass anyone to have it in their dustbin. I might as well be in Clacton on Sea wearing a string vest and hanky on my head--in fact maybe I will go there next year.

I was taking my time selecting gifts, and Dawn was getting very impatient; she pointed out we were supposed to be visiting the beach as well, not spending all day shopping. Number one: Dawn had no money, so she knew shopping wouldn't be much fun for her (though I did buy a small bottle of rum punch for her friend--I'm very generous sometimes, to a fault). Number two: with all her sun cream on, I'm sure Dawn would feel more comfortable out in the sun, rather than this cool environment. Number three: I expect there was no smoking in the store either.

While looking at the drinks wondering what to get Dad, I held up a bottle of the best Barbados rum--VQOR or something. As I did so, a man who looked astonishingly like Charles Aznavour, said to me that he's been all over the world, and:

"That is the best rum, the best in the world, believe me it is the best"

He said before continuing casually on his way. I didn't ask his opinion, it seemed he just had to tell me about it--maybe he recognized I knew nothing.

Dawn commented:

"Well there you are, you can't say better than that, he should know".

He was probably an old drunk--who looked like Charles Aznavour.

"Yes I'll have to get this one for Dad, plus a bottle of rum punch for me", I said. As it turned out, I gave the rum punch to dad as well.

I felt I needed to buy myself a t-shirt, but after

trying on one I liked with a picture of a big Bugs Bunny dressed Rasta style, in dreadlocks and large hat, then finding it didn't suit me very well, I gave up. Instead I chose a t-shirt for Ian's daughter Lucy, and Dawn picked another one with the legend 'Somebody who loves me bought me this t-shirt in Barbados' on it. Straight away Sarah wanted that--the rest of us liked it too. I found two nice tea towels for Mum, one with big, colourful pictures of Bajan birds, the other of native sea shells. Dawn's steely patience was wearing very thin by now, and she had gone outside the store to wait for me (I bet she was just having a fag).

When I got to the counter, it turned out I needed my passport to buy the tea towels at the duty-free price (these being one of a number of duty-free items). Of course I hadn't brought it, and this meant that from the price of £8 each I was expecting to pay, I could have got them duty-free for £4 each. It seemed sensible to buy them later at the airport duty-free shop (I took a gamble here, and was to be disappointed when arriving at the airport and finding I had lost my chance to purchase such nice towels because they were not even available there. That's what comes of looking after your money). I also decided to wait until then to buy the drinks. We hardly needed to carry big bottles of rum around with us on the beach for the rest of the day.

When I went outside with Michelle and Sarah, Dawn was nowhere to be seen. Surely she wouldn't just go off without me. I'll be easy prey for all the con-artists, they'll get my money without Dawn there

Chapter 13: 'We Do Like to Be Beside the Sea'

to protect me; how could she do this to me, my money, my money. As we walked towards the road, Dawn thankfully appeared from out of the shadows behind us, and we were a unit once again; leaving the merest hint of thick tar smoke hovering in a hidden space between two walls.

Walking along the road trying to keep in the shade, I saw the green and white police station--come museum and something else--just up ahead. This was the part we had visited a few days ago. There was a big drive through Kentucky fried chicken place before the station, and we trundled across its car park, over the grass to the beach. As soon as the girls hit the sand, they took their socks and shoes off. I jumped down and followed in their wake, with my socks and shoes still solidly on. I like to find somewhere to settle first.

Dawn, Michelle, and Sarah were going across a part of the beach which disappeared around a rock, and because you had to walk through the water, I didn't follow. I shouted out to Dawn, but herself and the children seemed to ignore me. I walked back to the road, planning to go further up and meet them on the other side. Reaching the road, I saw Dawn, Michelle, and Sarah coming off the beach onto the grass where we had first gone. Dawn said they couldn't get past the rock. Feeling a little grumpy at this time, I put Sarah under my arm--she had nothing on her feet except sand and water--and the four of us walked along the road until I recognized the place where we had joined the beach last time we were here.

Depositing Sarah with a certain amount of

relief, I looked around. There were a lot of people here today. They sit or lie in the sun, swim in the sea, and back on to the beach to sit or lie in the sun again. Now I think I'm going to get burnt because that's what happened the other day. We start walking along the beach towards the spot we found last time. The girls wade in the sea up to their ankles; I walk with a measured tread, careful not to get sand in my shoes. The small waves break and reach out onto the beach. Lady luck soon left me standing disgruntled in this paradise with wet shoes and socks on. It's as if the sea was saying, 'I told you so, why don't you take your socks and shoes off like everyone else--you're not in Bridgetown now?'

When we reached the spot from a few days before, we settled down on two sun beds Dawn took from nearby. They were the property of the hotel next to us, but no one ever said anything yet, so we don't worry about it too much. Well Dawn never does anyway, and she's the one who wants a sun bed in the first place. I don't intend to openly fry myself under the great yellow ball in the sky, so I sit on a rock or something; this way 'moi' can't be accused of stealing the sun beds--Dawn will rightly get all the blame.

I stood boldly in t-shirt and swimming trunks, then after applying sun lotion, hoped not to end up with Kentucky fried chicken legs later on. No harm in taking my shoes and socks off now--as they were both wet. It was very hot; I put a good dab of lotion on my nose and ventured into the sea. Michelle of course, was already in the water, and would stay there until it

Chapter 13: 'We Do Like to Be Beside the Sea'

was time to go. About a yard out there was a sudden dip in the seabed, and the stony bottom didn't help your footing much either; now and again I would stumble over when getting in or out of the water.

Sarah was too frightened to come in on her own, and when she was on the beach, ran down to the edge of the sea, and then ran up to where Dawn was a number of times. Sarah came into the water on a couple of occasions, but only because I was carrying her. She would cling to me all the time, not daring to let go. Sarah wasn't daft; when it was up to my chest, it would have been above her head, and as sure as I knew I couldn't walk on water and feed five thousand with a loaf of bread--she knew she couldn't swim. I wasn't 'Aqua-man' myself.

Michelle, Sarah, and me stayed talking and splashing in the sea. The waves sometimes washed over my head if I didn't bounce up at the right moment, then Sarah would splutter, asking to go back to the beach. She did a little swimming when I put my arms underneath her for support. Casually bouncing up and down with Sarah clinging to me, and Michelle nearby, chattering and splashing about, I revolved one way and then the other, feeling this very hot sun on my face. As I looked around, I could see some ships far out, but coming closer was a pesky Bajan jet ski tout. They always ask you if you want a ride. You feel like saying 'p*** off', but just say 'no thank you'.

Some people swim out to a small wooden platform anchored a hundred yards away. Now and again a water skier goes past. Further up from where we are, a large section of the beach is occupied by many people, most--if not all--are residents of the hotels there that back directly onto the sea.

Dawn is very much a sun worshipper today, seeming content to just lie back on her sun bed (courtesy of the hotel next door) and soak up some beneficial rays. Rather her than me, I'd feel like a beef burger under a grill. Dawn looks cool in shades and white nose. After a few visits to the water, I want to keep in the shade (of which there is very little) and dry out. A small tree provides some cover. I would like to let the children stay in the sea longer, but I'm getting uncomfortable, too much sun is making me want to stay in the shade all the time. I wait awhile, but we will have to go soon--for my sake.

The trickiest bit about leaving the beach in an orderly manner, apart from returning the sun beds without getting beaten with a piece of seaweed or a lump of flotsam for stealing them in the first place--in Dawn's case--is washing the sand from your feet and donning socks and shoes to once more become civilized. We have achieved this transformation with dexterity in the past, but every day is different. After clearing the sand off Sarah, she fell over and had to be washed down again. This annoyed Dawn, who was designated to take her back into the water. I didn't want to be so industrious; being in the sun wasn't encouraging me to sing 'Oh joy to the world and peace to all mankind'. I was content to dust sand off my feet, and then shove shoes and socks on to adopt the straining at the leash position.

Chapter 13: 'We Do Like to Be Beside the Sea'

As we left the beach, Michelle reminded me irritatingly that I had said we could eat out today for dinner. I replied in my most diplomatic manner I had indeed suggested it would be nice, but neither the less, had not said it was definite. The four of us crossed the road to wait patiently at the bus stop. Two minutes later we climbed aboard.

As usual at this time, 1630hr-1700hr, the bus was full. Sarah stood about three feet down, hidden amongst lower legs and shopping bags, though right next to me. The bus driver stops suddenly and pulls away quickly, so that if you're standing, you invariably swing from side to side trying to keep a grip on the handrail. Being tall and correspondingly gawky in my case, didn't help much either. I looked down at Sarah doing the same, though she could lean against my legs for support. I said to Dawn we could get some food at a big supermarket she had seen further on past our Black Rock bus stop.

We got off a few stops after the Esso garage. Dawn thought this place was just up the road, but in a while, with still no sign of the curiously elusive supermarket, we began to wonder. There were school children walking by us on the paths and waiting at the bus stops, laughing and joking with each other. Dawn and I were not really in this kind of mood ourselves--it had been another long day. Sarah was asleep; I had carried her since leaving the bus. I suggested we could search for the lost supermarket of Barbados a bit further, but Dawn--not needing much time to consider the options--said to leave it and turn back.

On the way, I noticed a little store, so we stopped and bought some bread rolls, potatoes, and fruit juice. It was a fair walk to Sandrift, taking us past a few of the small shack like bars Dawn had earlier guessed must be the equivalent of a pub. Before the main road is the locals' supermarket, so useful on our first night here--inhabited by the bulky Bajan man, who successfully managed to block each aisle, we tried to negotiate. The four of us crossed the main road, Dawn going back to the apartment, while I went with Michelle and Sarah to the Esso station to buy some donuts, and other goodies for us to eat, on this, our last night in good old Barbados (where the sun is big and always bright, and suckers like me are a welcome sight).

Michelle mentioned a couple of times that she would like to eat out, but Dawn and I had been content cooking our own dinners (well I did peel part of the big sweet potato at the Four Aces, before falling asleep). We also had financial considerations to keep in mind.

After a long day, upon returning to the apartment everyone has a shower. Especially necessary when you have been swimming in the sea and still carry sand on your person. Now with thoughts turning to our departure from this idyllic isle, I determine the timetable for tomorrow. Our flight is at 1845hr, but I will need to allow plenty of time to get to the airport. As we intend to go by bus, it will take a couple of hours at least. Dawn and I agree that if we are ready to leave the apartment by 1300hr--there will be no problem. I go to bed fairly early, as I always do. While I enter the world of dreams, Dawn, Michelle, and Sarah do what they always do--carry on talking and playing games.

Our expeditions on public transport, trying to keep us organized, all require a certain amount of effort on my part. During the day I hardly eat at all (so who's fault is that?), looking forward to a meal when we get back to the apartment. Slowly a veil comes down, and I float away quietly into the white walled corridors of my mind to catch a passing dream. How sweet is sleep, nature's way of recharging your batteries.

Chapter 14

'PARTING IS SUCH SWEET SORROW'

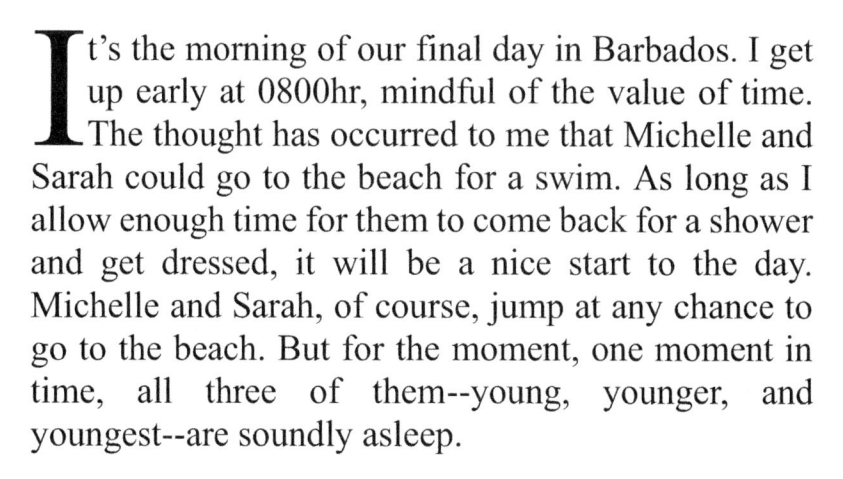

It's the morning of our final day in Barbados. I get up early at 0800hr, mindful of the value of time. The thought has occurred to me that Michelle and Sarah could go to the beach for a swim. As long as I allow enough time for them to come back for a shower and get dressed, it will be a nice start to the day. Michelle and Sarah, of course, jump at any chance to go to the beach. But for the moment, one moment in time, all three of them--young, younger, and youngest--are soundly asleep.

Dawn doesn't like to rise early. I put handfuls of bread out on the balcony for the always early birds. After breakfast I do most of the packing, leaving very little for later on. I don't touch Dawn's stuff--except to move it out of the way. However much time is set aside for meticulous plans, it often turns out to be not enough. With this understanding in mind, I proceed towards the middle hours of the morning in a cool and confident manner (poor, innocent fool that I am).

Sarah gets up next after me, as she always does, then Michelle; and I serve them both breakfasts. Dawn is not yet in the throes of leaving her bed--some sort of magnetism I suppose. It was about 1000hr when I decided to take Michelle and Sarah to the beach for their last frolic in the warm and friendly sea (it was on this side of the island anyway); under the blue, rolling skies of Barbados, with its golden orb sun looking down onto golden sands promising the holiday of a lifetime (except for certain days in the rainy season--as we found out). During the occasional unwanted reminders of wet and drizzly Britain, our English stiff upper lips and working class acceptance of adverse conditions came in handy.

Dawn had shown a flicker of concern with one eyelid when I first mentioned the trip, probably because she thought we didn't really have enough time, and could be late on our journey to the airport. As Dawn lay half asleep under an all-enveloping bed sheet, she listened with half an ear (unfortunate, but surely better than no ear at all) to me explaining that we were just on our way now, and wouldn't be very long. A murmuring in an unknown tongue, drifted through the door behind us--but wheels were in motion and spirits high, as we disappeared down the stairs.

I was pleased to be taking Michelle and Sarah to

the sea again, so they could enjoy themselves in the water, even on the day we were leaving. Luckily our flight was at 1845hr, and not in the morning; it gave us all day to reach the airport. The evening departure was certainly more suitable for Dawn. Michelle, myself, and our little brown Tinker bell--Sarah--walked happily down the hill; through the deserted Paradise Beach grounds, and then dropped off the low wall onto the beach.

Michelle and Sarah both ran into the sea, while I walked loosely and relaxed on the sand. Wearing shorts and t-shirt, I intended to stay dry--though the temptation to immerse myself in the luxurious warm water one more time was there. But this last visit to the beach was purely designed for the enjoyment of the children. I stood at various angles to the sun watching them. Sarah barely going in up to her knees, running back to the beach. Michelle, happy as always when she is in the sea.

'I hear the sound of waves all around me

Smiling, I swim over and under

Waves from the sea'

Two Bajan girls jog by us, the water lapping at their ankles. Further on, at the bend (where I had collected shells on the rocks), and just before the place we visited a few days ago, they stop and relax for a while, then start running slowly back again. It must be nearly an hour and a half before we return to the apartment.

Chapter 14: 'Parting is Such Sweet Sorrow'

Not much later Michelle and Sarah have showered and dressed. Michelle is wearing her killer whale t-shirt for the first time, and black leggings with Dr, Marten's. Although you don't see anybody else wearing D.M's in Barbados, I think she looks alright. They are practical for the remainder of our holiday. Sarah wears her loafers, leggings, and 'Somebody who loves me bought me this t-shirt in Barbados' t-shirt. Dawn was either still in bed or just getting up.

The four of us eventually finished packing all our belongings away, fairly squashing everything together tightly until it all went in. There was some food left, but not much. I put loads of bread on the balcony again. It was always gone in a short time because there are so many 'hungry' birds here in the surrounding trees. The birds really like us, but I notice if we don't put any food out for them--they never stay long.

During our stay we have somehow amassed about three thousand assorted bags, stuffing them in one of the little cupboards in the kitchen. All our washing up is done, I didn't think it fair to leave it for the manageress (though such is her disposition, she probably wouldn't mind). The four of us are ready to leave before one o'clock. I suppose the holidays over now, it's all systems go to catch the flight back home. Downstairs in the reception room, Dawn and I settle up our account. I give the lady extra payment for the glasses we have broken. Dawn just broke another one the day before, it's now three in all--why is it always her?

Dawn isn't too happy going by bus to the airport; she feels that the heavy suitcase, not to mention her heavy bag are a problem to carry, and there will be a lot of messing about changing buses at Bridgetown. I've no doubt she's right, but what must be done to save money, must be done. Dawn wants to order a taxi and go directly to the airport. The manageress tells us that if we go by bus, at Bridgetown there will be a long walk across town from the Jubilee side (near the post office) to the main station, from which the airport bound buses depart. I think I will be saving money somewhere, and suggest to Dawn it will be far too expensive travelling by taxi from Sandrift to the airport. Dawn says she is not feeling well (probably at the thought of taking a bus), and would really like to go by taxi. I tell Dawn diplomatically, that if she pays half the fare then I'll agree.

The manageress orders the taxi for 1415hr; its 1330hr now. Dawn, myself, Michelle, and Sarah go back upstairs to wait in the apartment. There is no pressure for us to vacate the room, as nobody is waiting to check in. Sometimes I wonder if anyone else ever does check in to be honest (but we quite liked it there). On reflection, paying for four on the buses and walking across Bridgetown with the bags, to catch another bus to the airport, does look a less attractive proposition than paying slightly extra for a taxi. Meanwhile, while waiting, we took a couple of photos and reflected on our holiday.

It felt much better sitting in a chair relaxing until transport arrived to whisk us off to our

Chapter 14: 'Parting is Such Sweet Sorrow'

destination. There would be no standing around sweating profusely at bus stops; no forced marches under a blistering sun; no parched throats or dizzy heads trying to plan the next step to oblivion (I'll kind of miss all that). No fear of being late for our flight--unless the car broke down of course. Then I heard the cab outside. What a wonderful holiday we had, what a wonderful time. It's sad, but now we have to go home.

Dawn wants to order a taxi and go directly to the airport

Dawn and I loaded our luggage into the boot, then Dawn asked the manageress if she would mind being in a picture. I took the photo, and as I do not appear in it, it is amongst the least frightening in the album. The manageress hoped we might stay at Sandrift again on another visit to Barbados. Dawn and

I both enthused we'd like to, but thinking afterwards, I said to her that it is more adventurous finding somewhere new to stay (anyway I would probably have tried the Casurina Beach Club next time, because of the good discount available to BA staff).

With a little wave goodbye, and happy, smiling faces, we were on our way. It's the last day here, Dawn hasn't got two pennies to rub together; I haven't got as good a suntan as I should have; the kids have seen the last of idyllic days by the sea for a long while; there still remains the tiny problem of securing seats for the flight home--where a return to work is all we can look forward to--and we're smiling?

The taxi takes us along the main highway to the airport. This just means a slightly wider road, which appears to be slightly straighter. I notice some buildings on our right. The driver informs me that they are accommodations for students attending the University nearby--not a hotel as I had assumed. I'm in a talkative mood during the trip, but our driver doesn't say an awful lot (though what he does say is awful). In the back seat everyone has fallen asleep. Was it something I said, or just the fact I said anything at all? Before long we arrive at the airport, and I have to pay the driver. The rather large gold ingot, worth thousands, will have to do--as I haven't got the kind of money he's asking for in cool cash. He'll probably retire now, and spend the rest of his life on holiday in Barbados, being far less hard up than we were.

Chapter

15

FEAR OF NOT FLYING

———✳———

Dawn, Michelle, Sarah, and myself make our way laboriously, suitcases and assorted bags in hand, to the departure area. There isn't a queue at the British Airways desk, so I check us in. All that remains now is to see whether we will be able to actually get on the plane later. The check-in staff tell me our chances are very good. There are two hours or more to wait before the witching hour begins, and standby staff crowd anxiously around the desk (in a most dignified way you understand); sweating like pigs to see who has drawn a short straw, who will suffer the ultimate rejection; heads dizzy with nausea as they slump to the cold, unsympathetic floor in a crumpled heap over their Carlton suitcases.

Then again, you could be one of those blessed by

Chapter 15: Fear of Not Flying

the hand of fate and get on the flight, if such manna from heaven is placed in your hands. A thin smile slowly grows on your smug face; cold sweat rapidly disappears to be replaced by a warm glow. At this shining star of a moment, this triumphant fanfare feeling of good cheer, you don't give a flicked bread crumb for the others--tough luck if they lie whimpering in your dust, sobbing their hearts out at the injustice of it all. You in capital letters are on, and that's just about the size of it. Stepping gingerly over the crumpled, squealing bodies, you head with an exaggerated swagger towards the boarding gate. But such a wonderful or alternately hellish experience is yet to come for us--we are in the early stages of the ritual of the standby staff.

There are still some gifts to buy before leaving the laid back land of Barbados. I look in a few of the airport shops only yards away. Three are souvenir stores, another two selling mostly food or stationary. I ponder on getting Mum some tea towels, but there aren't any as nice as those in Cave Shepherd (that I didn't buy). Dad always appreciates something to drink; this can be obtained from the duty-free inside. I'm still looking for a gift for Mercy. Michelle wants to buy something for her Europhil Drama School friends. I didn't think it wise to give her too much money because our family is the main consideration. In the end, after much hassle between us, Michelle is satisfied with her modest purchases.

While we were sitting patiently, somewhat idly waiting, Michelle bought a big bag of chips--which were very tasty according to Dawn. Nobody had much chance to eat many though, as for some reason Michelle dropped the lot on the spotless, smooth floor of the departure area. A cleaner nonchalantly came along and swept them up. I said to Michelle I had bought the chips she'd wanted, what she did with them was up to her. Michelle wasn't happy with this explanation of course, and kept coming over to ask for more chips, harassing me in front of fine, upstanding people quietly sitting with their pristine, well behaved children. The second bag of chips went down well enough, this time held tightly in Michelle's otter like clutches.

While Michelle was eating, I stood by the check in desk with about thirty other staff. The cool, relaxed, courageous image on show to the world was fake. The very least you could say was that we were anxious, our breath extremely bated, ears and eyes tuned to the slightest flicker of movement, or lowest level of sound. A pin dropping would have shattered the almost eerie silence. Every hair on my head was nervous, prepared to stand on end at the very mention of the 'sorry' word. It seemed like hours I stood transfixed to the spot, a solitary fly buzzing nearby.

It was almost time for the flight to go--let alone time to start calling those who have sun shining from obscure places forward. With about fifteen minutes to departure, the check in staff began to form a few words, a couple of names. Good God, there were only another thirty people, what about the rest of us you spuds--what about meee? Was I doomed? A few hours ago when I had checked in, the girl had said it was looking good.

Chapter 15: Fear of Not Flying

Now it wasn't looking good to me--unless I had missed something here besides a few heartbeats--so what were they playing at? I had lost two pounds in sweat and gone nearly bald and grey worrying about my chances of ever leaving this little island before Labour got back in power (believe me that could be a long time). Bottom line; I was brave--but A Man Called Horse had it easier.

Luckily once again, as at Gatwick, my name was called out quickly, about third or fourth. One could feel the envy of the others burning into one, as one gleefully collected the boarding passes and walked humbly over to Dawn, Michelle, and Sarah to tell them the good news. As for those I left behind me, I could spare no interest in their fate--they would have done the same for me.

Dawn--as at Gatwick--could have gone through earlier because of her firm ticket, but she decided to wait with us to make sure we all travelled together. The boarding gate was in the duty-free area. Everybody stood around with time to kill, as our flight would now be late departing. Here was my opportunity to buy some duty-free. Before long my trophy bag consisted of a bottle of the best rum for Dad, rum punch for me, and some tea towels for Mum--though still not as good as those in Cave Shepherd...never mind. I couldn't find a suitable gift for Mercy. I gazed goggled eyed at all the perfumes, not really knowing what I was looking at. They didn't have price tags, and I was scared to ask in case it turned out to be around fifty pounds each time (I could never afford that kind of money--unless it was her Christmas present). Michelle wanted a book costing £5 or more. I passed on that, but bought Dawn a small bottle of rum punch she wanted for a friend.

Before long everybody shuffled up the gangway and through the aircraft door into an object of technical wonder. The London flight was running approximately one hour late (not much wonder there). Myself, Michelle, and Sarah sat in three seats on the left side of the plane, next to the window. This was a good arrangement, as we were altogether and could see out into the clouds, and down at the miniature landscape of the Lilliputian world below. Also, each time one of us wanted to get out of their seat, they would not be disturbing other people. Dawn was in her element, soaking up the smog in the ghetto like smoking section--so everybody was happy.

As usual I felt my legs very restricted, having only millimeters of space to move in. You wouldn't get this problem in first class or even club class, but I know my place, and usually it was in economy. This time though it seemed a little more inconvenient than usual (now we're talking really inconvenient), and low and behold, at the end of the flight, nearly eight hours later, the person in front of me pushed his seat back to the forward position. If I'd realized this nuisance had pushed his seat back into me at the very beginning of our flight, I would have asked him politely to move it forward for a spell or two. If that failed because his sense of common decency was lower than a snake's belly at the bottom of the Pacific, then I would probably find--for some unknown reason--my hands and feet frequently, and alternately, banging with

Chapter 15: Fear of Not Flying

varying degrees of intensity against the back of his seat, unfortunately making it impossible for him to relax. What a shame. But I had not known about his inconsiderate action, and sat cooped up like a corn fed shed chicken throughout the flight.

As I settled in my seat with headphones on, Michelle told me hers were not working properly, I gave mine to Michelle and went to ask a steward for another pair. Sitting down again, I unwrapped the new headphones and put them on--but they snapped in half as I did so. It was back to the steward, who laughed and said 'third time lucky'.

Michelle and Sarah don't want all their food (just as they didn't on the flight out from Gatwick), so I had plenty to eat. Every now and again Dawn came over to visit us, but couldn't stay long, as it was hard on her lungs breathing in a smoke free zone. Dawn appeared to be a little happier on the flight going back than coming out. It was probably due to her not having a cold now, and the blissful experience of being seated in the smog filled smoking section.

Browsing through the Highlife magazine, I came across a couple of perfumes in the duty-free gifts section that were around £15 each. I thought Mercy might like one called 'Beautiful'. When they flounced down the aisles selling duty-free later, I bought it for her. The stewardess astonished me by asking if I wanted anything else. What do they think I am--made of money? Dawn of course, bought nothing--how could she? Since the beginning of our last day in Barbados it would have been physically impossible. Relatively speaking, we were both in the same boat; although literally speaking, we were on the same plane.

The flight passed uneventfully--which is always a good thing--and in a short while our wheels touched down on the familiar ground of mother England. Everyone, with tears in their eyes, sang lustily 'there'll always be an England', and bottom lips trembled with the emotion of it all. 'Back to bloody work tomorrow' most of them thought (some of course, like royalty, most millionaires, all estate agents, all solicitors, chief executives and people asking you for money in the Tesco's car park…) don't suffer with the same affliction those common to the usual system have thrust upon them; they simply don't need to work, or the work they do hardly requires any effort; or they've no intention of ever engaging in such a deeply unappealing activity anyway). I wasn't back at work tomorrow, neither was Dawn. This beast of burden still lay lurking, like a huge shadow cast over our imminent future. All things come to pass, including holidays.

Seated in the smog filled smoking section

Chapter 15: Fear of Not Flying

For the time being though, everybody was standing in the aisles expecting the door to open so we could all get off, then run as fast as possible to passport control and the baggage reclaim hall; after which it was easy peasy--unless you were caught smuggling. I seemed to stand there for hours, maybe it was. They only have to open the door; it has a handle like any other door. All the time I'm thinking (while I'm not thinking 'there'll always be an England'), I've got to block the aisle while Michelle and Sarah get out, so we can walk off together. He looks like he might push in quick; I'll have to watch him. Somehow it seems as if you've been standing up longer than you've been sitting down--and that was eight and a half hours.

Suddenly nostrils dilate to the whiff of fresh air, and the passengers--like bulls--charge for the exit. The open doorway is like a red handkerchief being held up in front of their wild eyes. Everybody smiles at everyone else--why, the holiday's over, what is there to smile about--going back to work tomorrow? For the first time on the flight, the cabin crew smile at us--because they're saying goodbye and are glad to be rid of you.

Chapter
16

RETURN OF THE NATIVES

After negotiating passport control and being allowed back into the country (priority is given to those seeking free housing, money, and additional benefits eagerly provided by a doting British government), Dawn makes a quick phone call to Mum and Dad to say we've arrived safely. I move swiftly on to baggage reclaim, but Dawn wants to stop for a while for a smoke. Why it must have been minutes since the last one. I'm a little impatient about this and bite the bullet until we're back on course again.

At the baggage reclaim, Michelle thought she saw our suitcase going around on the belt, but it was somebody else's. Once we were ready to go, a young woman intruded upon us with a passengers'

Chapter 16: Return of the Natives

questionnaire. It posed trivia questions such as, 'was the service on the flight satisfactory?' and giving me a choice between good, fair, average, or poor for each answer. Of course, the service is always very unsatisfactory, you can't get off the plane when you want to, you have to sit down for hours, you can't get any privacy, have to join a long queue just to go to the toilet--and when you do get in, it's too small for anyone who isn't a Slim Fast midget. These are a few of the disadvantages that come to mind, but as I'm BA staff, I replied it was mostly good. As they say in The X-files, 'the truth is out there' (flying through the clouds at this very moment). I was feeling very relaxed and laid back after the holiday, so this impertinent intrusion on our valuable time did not annoy me as it normally would have done.

Pushing a trolley loaded with baggage, I staggered wearily through the 'Nothing To Declare' exit, and the four of us joined other jet lagged, hang dog expressional world travellers pouring out into the arrivals terminal building; with ranks of beady, gleaming, swiveling eyes looking us all up and down, searching for faces they knew. Nobody was waiting for us--so we were getting looked at for nothing.

The next stage of our plan involved phoning for a taxi to take us to Dawn's place, then Dawn would drive myself and the children round to Ian and Julie's to pick up my car. Firstly though, Dawn and I wanted to get some money. Our flight to London had actually taken place during the night, so I had effectively gone a day without sleep. Michelle and Sarah slept on the flight (Sarah quite a long time), and were therefore not too bad. I don't know about Dawn. Michelle wanted something to eat (after all that was served on the plane), and I bought her sweets. Sarah asked for a Mars bar, but--not unusually for her--didn't eat it all.

Surrounding us was a metropolis of shops, clothing, leather goods, lots of ties (as always), more or less anything; though a bank or cash machine was hard to find. The predicament seemed worse because I was so tired and just wanted to get home. Eventually, on our immediate horizon, a couple of cash machines appeared. Dawn found she could not get money out with her card, but I withdrew sixty pounds on my Midland, which was surely enough to cover the taxi fare home. From the cash point we went over to the public phones nearby, so Dawn, with her telephone operator voice, could arrange for a taxi. Dawn found a couple of local taxi services, and upon ringing the first, told me the cost would be £55. Both of us thought that too high. Fortunately, the second number Dawn rang provided a more acceptable figure of £40, which was agreed to on the spot.

As we made our way outside to a pick-up point, a svelte, expensive limousine pulled up nearby, undoubtedly waiting for passengers with money. Out of the four of us, I was the only one with money, £60--but it was better than nothing. It didn't take long for me to realize that this four wheeled lap of luxury was not the transport Dawn had ordered. Our taxi arrived minutes later--a ropey old estate with dull, weather beaten paint work, and a fragile appearance, which suggested the

Chapter 16: Return of the Natives

doors, might drop off one by one at any moment. For a few seconds, as I blinked away the tiredness in my eyes, the registration plate seemed to read 'clapped out'. But we weren't complaining--with a bit of luck it would get us home.

Dawn and I had contemplated the various other options of transport, and had decided for what we would spend on trains and buses etc. (the coach service took you to London, Victoria); we might as well go directly by taxi. With the luggage loaded safely in the back, and the four of us seated snugly in the front we were ready to roll. The driver told me that it was better for him to take another route to Heathrow, rather than use the motorway, which he would normally do; the reason being, at this time of day there was so much traffic. For a moment I thought we'd end up going all around the houses in ever increasing circles--and paying an increased charge to match the circles. It seemed we did go on a tour of Britain, but the fare had been fixed at £40, so it turned out okay. Dawn and I were quite pleased the taxi dropped us at the entrance to Hillingdon Hospital's maternity wing, which was opposite Dawn's flat across the road.

I helped Dawn carry her bags upstairs, Sarah came with me. Michelle waited downstairs, outside. It was the first time I had seen Dawn's quarters (and did I laugh), consisting of a shared kitchen and bathroom plus two rooms--a bedroom and a sitting room--being for her use only. It seemed a bit odd, as the two rooms were opposite each other with a corridor in between. When leaving one room, Dawn had to lock the door, and then cross the corridor to enter the other one.

We went downstairs again to load the luggage into Dawn's car. As I entered the car, there was a splashing sound around my feet; which naturally, was caused by a small lake situated on the floor--passenger's side--of Dawn's vehicle. From where I was sitting, this distant relation to Lake Windermere would make the car more suitable as a bird sanctuary for a family of mallard ducks, than a method of traversing dry land. The water was a rusty brown in colour, and had managed to infiltrate my socks to a modest degree.

As I put my safety belt on, I mentioned the lake to Dawn, who said she had meant to get it fixed. Ian had suggested drilling a hole in the floor, so the water could run out. A pity the hole had not been drilled already I thought, as I shifted my feet slightly. Apparently it had been like that for a while, but according to Dawn this was a good little car. I'm sure it was, though the rusty water may not have been to everyone's liking. I was too tired to drill a hole myself right now, and so braved the fury of the elements rising up around me. The only real danger, I concluded, would be if I slipped down too far out of my seat and started to drown.

Dawn said that Mum and Dad would be around old Nan's, as they normally go there on Thursdays. She thought we could say hello, and give Dad his drinks before moving on to Ian and Julie's to pick up my car. On the way to Nan's, I lent Dawn some money for petrol, but said I wanted it back soon--when could I

Chapter 16: Return of the Natives

have it? This did not go down too well, and Dawn became annoyed, displaying gnashing teeth over the steering wheel, as her temper slowly got the upper hand over her naturally calm demeanor. When she turned to me, I thought flames were going to come from her mouth--but thankfully it was only words:

"Don't worry, you'll get it back--don't you think I'm going to pay you or something?" she said angrily (just because she hasn't got any money)

We were both tired. Dawn parked up outside old Nan's house, and the rusty brown lido rippled around my feet.

I felt a bit guilty, not having bought old Nan a present. Dawn got out to knock on the door. Nan appeared at the doorstep, and waved to us as we stayed in the car. I felt myself slide down in the seat a little, but quickly got back up--not being a good swimmer. Dawn returned and told me she had explained to Nan we were all tired and had come around to see if Mum and Dad were there. But they were not. Dawn then remembered Mum and Dad planned to come down Friday or Saturday to Ian and Julie's--so had decided against Thursday for Nan's. I said:

"Didn't you just know that would happen, the one Thursday we would like them to be here, they change to another day"

Dawn's car pulled away, with me still complaining, and headed for a small detached bungalow somewhere in Iver, Bucks. Soon we arrived at Ian and Julie's home, and there outside, by the kerb, was my car as I had left it--unwashed. Ian wasn't in, Julie gave me the keys, and being so anxious to get some sleep, after a brief chat, I gave her the t-shirt for Lucy and we went on our way again.

Dawn asked me to follow her back to the hospital, in case she ran out of fuel. Also it seemed her car was rapidly filling up with water and sinking fast. Before long it would go down in a swirl of bubbles, with maybe only a few cassettes floating in the flotsam over the spot where the car had last been seen. When Dawn was safely outside the hospital, I drove on towards our lonely house. As we passed the Top Rank bingo (a kind of temple for so many), Michelle was sick in one of our shopping bags. Maybe it was an omen--that bingo can make you sick. I feel sick sometimes thinking how much it costs for Mercy to play.

Going across the roundabout on the Hayes by-pass, near our house, we saw Ian coming from the Hayes Town side. Ian followed us home. Luckily, when I arrived there was a place to park. Mercy was not in. I assumed she had gone to work, but un-be known to me, she had in-fact been unwell for more than a week, and was staying at Belinda's (a friend of ours). Ian came in for a cup of tea, but soon left as he was working. Sitting in the house with all our bags and suitcases on the floor, I said to Michelle and Sarah they should go to bed, get some sleep.

I was very tired, but still found myself sorting out the dirty clothes, putting toothbrushes and washing

Chapter 16: Return of the Natives

items back in the bathroom, creating some kind of order out of the chaos, before giving in to the desire for sleep that beckoned me ever closer. Finally I lay my head down on the pillow, slowly submerging blissfully into an all-encompassing world of colourful thoughts. In my mind our holiday still lived, in bouncing browns, brilliant whites, and rippling blues; everybody said, 'alright?', 'alright', throughout a landscape of green in varying hues. Barbados was a world away--but we can still dream.

THE END...FOR NOW

ACKNOWLEDGEMENTS

BA Staff Travel: For letting us on the flights out to Barbados and back again, so we could have our holiday.

Dawn: Without whom there would obviously have been a lot less biting, satirical, Mickey taking comments (which I enjoy).

My daughters, Michelle and Sarah: For behaving themselves well on the holiday and thereby helping me from suffering undue amounts of stress.

The manageress of Sandrift Apartments: For being such a wonderful host to us while we were there; the genuine face of Bajan hospitality.

The old bat in St Lawrence: For single handedly providing us with a prime example of the kind of people who will take advantage of you in life if you're not careful.

Last and certainly least--Barbados taxi drivers: For showing us that the Serengeti vultures are maybe not so bad after all--compared to them.

Printed in Great Britain
by Amazon